Contents

ROASTED VEGETABLES

Servings: 12 | Prep: 15m | Cooks: 40m | Total: 55m

NUTRITION FACTS

Calories: 123 | Carbohydrates: 20g | Fat: 4.7g | Protein: 2g | Cholesterol: 0mg

INGREDIENTS

- 1 small butternut squash, cubed
- 1 tablespoon chopped fresh thyme
- 2 red bell peppers, seeded and diced
- 2 tablespoons chopped fresh rosemary
- 1 sweet potato, peeled and cubed
- 1/4 cup olive oil
- 3 Yukon Gold potatoes, cubed
- 2 tablespoons balsamic vinegar
- 1 red onion, quartered
- salt and freshly ground black pepper

DIRECTIONS

1. Preheat oven to 475 degrees F (245 degrees C).
2. In a large bowl, combine the squash, red bell peppers, sweet potato, and Yukon Gold potatoes. Separate the red onion quarters into pieces, and add them to the mixture.
3. In a small bowl, stir together thyme, rosemary, olive oil, vinegar, salt, and pepper. Toss with vegetables until they are coated. Spread evenly on a large roasting pan.
4. Roast for 35 to 40 minutes in the preheated oven, stirring every 10 minutes, or until vegetables are cooked through and browned.

UNBELIEVABLE CHICKEN

Servings: 6 | Prep: 15m | Cooks: 20m | Total: 9h | Additional: 8h25m

NUTRITION FACTS

Calories: 337 | Carbohydrates: 22.4g | Fat: 16.4g | Protein: 24.8g | Cholesterol: 67mg

INGREDIENTS

- 1/4 cup cider vinegar
- 1/2 cup brown sugar
- 3 tablespoons prepared coarse-ground mustard
- 1 1/2 teaspoons salt

- 3 cloves garlic, peeled and minced
- ground black pepper to taste
- 1 lime, juiced
- 6 tablespoons olive oil
- 1/2 lemon, juiced
- 6 skinless, boneless chicken breast halves

DIRECTIONS

1. In a large glass bowl, mix the cider vinegar, mustard, garlic, lime juice, lemon juice, brown sugar, salt, and pepper. Whisk in the olive oil. Place chicken in the mixture. Cover, and marinate 8 hours, or overnight.
2. Preheat an outdoor grill for high heat.
3. Lightly oil the grill grate. Place chicken on the prepared grill, and cook 6 to 8 minutes per side, until juices run clear. Discard marinade.

LEMON GARLIC TILAPIA

Servings: 4 | Prep: 10m | Cooks: 30m | Total: 40m

NUTRITION FACTS

Calories: 142 | Carbohydrates: 1.4g | Fat: 4.4g | Protein: 23.1g | Cholesterol: 49mg

INGREDIENTS

- 4 tilapia fillets
- 1 clove garlic, finely chopped
- 3 tablespoons fresh lemon juice
- 1 teaspoon dried parsley flakes
- 1 tablespoon butter, melted
- pepper to taste

DIRECTIONS

1. Preheat oven to 375 degrees F (190 degrees C). Spray a baking dish with non-stick cooking spray.
2. Rinse tilapia fillets under cool water, and pat dry with paper towels.
3. Place fillets in baking dish. Pour lemon juice over fillets, then drizzle butter on top. Sprinkle with garlic, parsley, and pepper.
4. Bake in preheated oven until the fish is white and flakes when pulled apart with a fork, about 30 minutes.

SPAGHETTI SQUASH

Servings: 6 | Prep: 15m | Cooks: 30m | Total: 45m

NUTRITION FACTS

Calories: 147 | Carbohydrates: 12.8g | Fat: 9.8g | Protein: 4.1g | Cholesterol: 17mg

INGREDIENTS

- 1 spaghetti squash, halved lengthwise and seeded
- 1 1/2 cups chopped tomatoes
- 2 tablespoons vegetable oil
- 3/4 cup crumbled feta cheese
- 1 onion, chopped
- 3 tablespoons sliced black olives
- 1 clove garlic, minced
- 2 tablespoons chopped fresh basil

DIRECTIONS

1. Preheat oven to 350 degrees F (175 degrees C). Lightly grease a baking sheet.
2. Place spaghetti squash with cut sides down on the prepared baking sheet, and bake 30 minutes in the preheated oven, or until a sharp knife can be inserted with only a little resistance. Remove squash from oven and set aside to cool enough to be easily handled.
3. Meanwhile, heat oil in a skillet over medium heat. Cook and stir onion in oil until tender. Add garlic; cook and stir until fragrant, 2 to 3 minutes. Stir in tomatoes and cook until tomatoes are warmed through.
4. Use a large spoon to scoop the stringy pulp from the squash and place in a medium bowl. Toss with the vegetables, feta cheese, olives, and basil. Serve warm.

HONEY ROASTED RED POTATOES

Servings: 4 | Prep: 10m | Cooks: 35m | Total: 45m

NUTRITION FACTS

Calories: 156 | Carbohydrates: 23.4g | Fat: 6.2g | Protein: 2.5g | Cholesterol: 15mg

INGREDIENTS

- 1 pound red potatoes, quartered
- 1 teaspoon dry mustard
- 2 tablespoons diced onion
- 1 pinch salt
- 2 tablespoons butter, melted
- 1 pinch ground black pepper

- 1 tablespoon honey

DIRECTIONS

1. Preheat oven to 375 degrees F (190 degrees C). Lightly coat an 11x7 inch baking dish with nonstick cooking spray.
2. Bake in the preheated 375 degrees F (190 degrees C) oven for 35 minutes or until tender, stirring halfway through the cooking time.

SLOW COOKER CILANTRO LIME CHICKEN
Servings: 6 | Prep: 10m | Cooks: 4h | Total: 4h10m

NUTRITION FACTS

Calories: 272 | Carbohydrates: 9.3g | Fat: 4.7g | Protein: 45.3g | Cholesterol: 117mg

INGREDIENTS

- 1 (16 ounce) jar salsa
- 3 tablespoons chopped fresh cilantro
- 1 (1.25 ounce) package dry taco seasoning mix
- 3 pounds skinless, boneless chicken breast halves
- 1 lime, juiced

DIRECTIONS

1. Place the salsa, taco seasoning, lime juice, and cilantro into a slow cooker, and stir to combine. Add the chicken breasts, and stir to coat with the salsa mixture. Cover the cooker, set to High, and cook until the chicken is very tender, about 4 hours. If desired, set cooker to Low and cook 6 to 8 hours. Shred chicken with 2 forks to serve.

PENNE WITH CHICKEN AND ASPARAGUS
Servings: 8 | Prep: 15m | Cooks: 20m | Total: 35m

NUTRITION FACTS

Calories: 332 | Carbohydrates: 43.3g | Fat: 10.9g | Protein: 16.7g | Cholesterol: 20mg

INGREDIENTS

- 1 (16 ounce) package dried penne pasta
- 1/2 cup low-sodium chicken broth
- 5 tablespoons olive oil, divided

- 1 bunch slender asparagus spears, trimmed, cut on diagonal into 1-inch pieces
- 2 skinless, boneless chicken breast halves - cut into cubes
- 1 clove garlic, thinly sliced
- salt and pepper to taste
- 1/4 cup Parmesan cheese
- garlic powder to taste

DIRECTIONS

1. Bring a large pot of lightly salted water to boil. Add pasta, and cook until al dente, about 8 to 10 minutes. Drain, and set aside.
2. Warm 3 tablespoons olive oil in a large skillet over medium-high heat. Stir in chicken, and season with salt, pepper, and garlic powder. Cook until chicken is cooked through and browned, about 5 minutes. Remove chicken to paper towels.
3. Pour chicken broth into the skillet. Then stir in asparagus, garlic, and a pinch more garlic powder, salt, and pepper. Cover, and steam until the asparagus is just tender, about 5 to 10 minutes. Return chicken to the skillet, and warm through.
4. Stir chicken mixture into pasta, and mix well. Let sit about 5 minutes. Drizzle with 2 tablespoons olive oil, stir again, then sprinkle with Parmesan cheese.

SLOW COOKER TURKEY BREAST

Servings: 12 | Prep: 10m | Cooks: 8h | Total: 8h10m

NUTRITION FACTS

Calories: 273 | Carbohydrates: 1.5g | Fat: 1.5g | Protein: 59.5g | Cholesterol: 164mg

INGREDIENTS

- 1 (6 pound) bone-in turkey breast
- 1 (1 ounce) envelope dry onion soup mix

DIRECTIONS

1. Rinse the turkey breast and pat dry. Cut off any excess skin, but leave the skin covering the breast. Rub onion soup mix all over outside of the turkey and under the skin. Place in a slow cooker. Cover, and cook on High for 1 hour, then set to Low, and cook for 7 hours.

KICKIN' COLLARD GREENS

Servings: 6 | Prep: 10m | Cooks: 1h | Total: 1h10m

NUTRITION FACTS

Calories: 127 | Carbohydrates: 7.9g | Fat: 9.2g | Protein: 4.4g | Cholesterol: 12mg

INGREDIENTS

- 1 tablespoon olive oil
- 1 teaspoon pepper
- 3 slices bacon
- 3 cups chicken broth
- 1 large onion, chopped
- 1 pinch red pepper flakes
- 2 cloves garlic, minced
- 1 pound fresh collard greens, cut into 2-inch pieces
- 1 teaspoon salt

DIRECTIONS

1. Heat oil in a large pot over medium-high heat. Add bacon, and cook until crisp. Remove bacon from pan, crumble and return to the pan. Add onion, and cook until tender, about 5 minutes. Add garlic, and cook until just fragrant. Add collard greens, and fry until they start to wilt.
2. Pour in chicken broth, and season with salt, pepper, and red pepper flakes. Reduce heat to low, cover, and simmer for 45 minutes, or until greens are tender.

PRETZEL TURTLES

Servings: 20 | Prep: 10m | Cooks: 4m | Total: 14m

NUTRITION FACTS

Calories: 82 | Carbohydrates: 14.1g | Fat: 2.2g | Protein: 1.7g | Cholesterol: 1mg

INGREDIENTS

- 20 small mini pretzels
- 20 pecan halves
- 20 chocolate covered caramel candies

DIRECTIONS

1. Preheat oven to 300 degrees F (150 degrees C).
2. Arrange the pretzels in a single layer on a parchment lined cookie sheet. Place one chocolate covered caramel candy on each pretzel.
3. Bake for 4 minutes. While the candy is warm, press a pecan half onto each candy covered pretzel. Cool completely before storing in an airtight container.

ROASTED GARLIC LEMON BROCCOLI

Servings: 6 | Prep: 10m | Cooks: 15m | Total: 25m

NUTRITION FACTS

Calories: 49 | Carbohydrates: 7g | Fat: 1.9g | Protein: 2.9g | Cholesterol: 0mg

INGREDIENTS

- 2 heads broccoli, separated into florets
- 1/2 teaspoon ground black pepper
- 2 teaspoons extra-virgin olive oil
- 1 clove garlic, minced
- 1 teaspoon sea salt
- 1/2 teaspoon lemon juice

DIRECTIONS

1. Preheat the oven to 400 degrees F (200 degrees C).
2. In a large bowl, toss broccoli florets with the extra virgin olive oil, sea salt, pepper and garlic. Spread the broccoli out in an even layer on a baking sheet.
3. Bake in the preheated oven until florets are tender enough to pierce the stems with a fork, 15 to 20 minutes. Remove and transfer to a serving platter. Squeeze lemon juice liberally over the broccoli before serving for a refreshing, tangy finish.

AUTHENTIC GERMAN POTATO SALAD

Servings: 4 | Prep: 30m | Cooks: 20m | Total: 50m

NUTRITION FACTS

Calories: 183 | Carbohydrates: 32.2g | Fat: 3.9g | Protein: 5.4g | Cholesterol: 10mg

INGREDIENTS

- 3 cups diced peeled potatoes
- 3 tablespoons white sugar
- 4 slices bacon
- 1 teaspoon salt
- 1 small onion, diced
- 1/8 teaspoon ground black pepper
- 1/4 cup white vinegar
- 1 tablespoon chopped fresh parsley
- 2 tablespoons water

DIRECTIONS

1. Place the potatoes into a pot, and fill with enough water to cover. Bring to a boil, and cook for about 10 minutes, or until easily pierced with a fork. Drain, and set aside to cool.
2. Place the bacon in a large deep skillet over medium-high heat. Fry until browned and crisp, turning as needed. Remove from the pan and set aside.
3. Add onion to the bacon grease, and cook over medium heat until browned. Add the vinegar, water, sugar, salt and pepper to the pan. Bring to a boil, then add the potatoes and parsley. Crumble in half of the bacon. Heat through, then transfer to a serving dish. Crumble the remaining bacon over the top, and serve warm.

RED LENTIL CURRY

Servings: 8 | Prep: 10m | Cooks: 30m | Total: 40m

NUTRITION FACTS

Calories: 192 | Carbohydrates: 32.5g | Fat: 2.6g | Protein: 12.1g | Cholesterol: 0mg

INGREDIENTS

- 2 cups red lentils
- 1 teaspoon chili powder
- 1 large onion, diced
- 1 teaspoon salt
- 1 tablespoon vegetable oil
- 1 teaspoon white sugar
- 2 tablespoons curry paste
- 1 teaspoon minced garlic
- 1 tablespoon curry powder
- 1 teaspoon minced fresh ginger
- 1 teaspoon ground turmeric
- 1 (14.25 ounce) can tomato puree
- 1 teaspoon ground cumin

DIRECTIONS

1. Wash the lentils in cold water until the water runs clear. Put lentils in a pot with enough water to cover; bring to a boil, place a cover on the pot, reduce heat to medium-low, and simmer, adding water during cooking as needed to keep covered, until tender, 15 to 20 minutes. Drain.
2. Heat vegetable oil in a large skillet over medium heat; cook and stir onions in hot oil until caramelized, about 20 minutes.
3. Mix curry paste, curry powder, turmeric, cumin, chili powder, salt, sugar, garlic, and ginger together in a large bowl; stir into the onions. Increase heat to high and cook, stirring constantly, until fragrant, 1 to 2 minutes.

4. Stir in the tomato puree, remove from heat and stir into the lentils.

PORK CHOPS FOR THE SLOW COOKER

Servings: 6 | Prep: 5m | Cooks: 6h | Total: 6h5m

NUTRITION FACTS

Calories: 146 | Carbohydrates: 10.6g | Fat: 4.3g | Protein: 16g | Cholesterol: 36mg

INGREDIENTS

- 6 boneless pork chops
- 1/4 cup ketchup
- 1/4 cup brown sugar
- 2 cloves garlic, crushed
- 1 teaspoon ground ginger
- salt and pepper to taste
- 1/2 cup soy sauce

DIRECTIONS

1. Place pork chops in slow cooker. Combine remaining ingredients and pour over pork chops.
2. Cook on Low setting for 6 hours, until internal temperature of pork has reached 145 degrees F (63 degrees C).

BASIL CHICKEN OVER ANGEL HAIR

Servings: 4 | Prep: 15m | Cooks: 20m | Total: 35m

NUTRITION FACTS

Calories: 362 | Carbohydrates: 37.8g | Fat: 10.8g | Protein: 28.4g | Cholesterol: 57mg

INGREDIENTS

- 1 (8 ounce) package angel hair pasta
- 2 cups boneless chicken breast halves, cooked and cubed
- 2 teaspoons olive oil
- 1/4 cup chopped fresh basil
- 1/2 cup finely chopped onion
- 1/2 teaspoon salt
- 1 clove garlic, chopped
- 1/8 teaspoon hot pepper sauce

- 2 1/2 cups chopped tomatoes
- 1/4 cup Parmesan cheese

DIRECTIONS

1. In a large pot of salted boiling water, cook angel hair pasta until it is al dente, about 8 to 10 minutes. Drain, and set aside.
2. In a large skillet, heat oil over medium-high heat. Saute the onions and garlic. Stir in the tomatoes, chicken, basil, salt and hot pepper sauce. Reduce heat to medium, and cover skillet. Simmer for about 5 minutes, stirring frequently, until mixture is hot and tomatoes are soft.
3. Toss sauce with hot cooked angel hair pasta to coat. Serve with Parmesan cheese.

GARLIC GREEN BEANS

Servings: 5 | Prep: 10m | Cooks: 15m | Total: 25m

NUTRITION FACTS

Calories: 157 | Carbohydrates: 9.3g | Fat: 11.9g | Protein: 4g | Cholesterol: 11mg

INGREDIENTS

- 1 tablespoon butter
- 2 (14.5 ounce) cans green beans, drained
- 3 tablespoons olive oil
- salt and pepper to taste
- 1 medium head garlic - peeled and sliced
- 1/4 cup grated Parmesan cheese

DIRECTIONS

1. In a large skillet over medium heat, melt butter with olive oil; add garlic, and cook until lightly browned, stirring frequently. Stir in green beans, and season with salt and pepper. Cook until beans are tender, about 10 minutes. Remove from heat, and sprinkle with Parmesan cheese.

BLACK BEANS AND RICE

Servings: 10 | Prep: 5m | Cooks: 25m | Total: 30m

NUTRITION FACTS

Calories: 140 | Carbohydrates: 27.1g | Fat: 0.9g | Protein: 6.3g | Cholesterol: 0mg

INGREDIENTS

- 1 teaspoon olive oil
- 1 1/2 cups low sodium, low fat vegetable broth
- 1 onion, chopped
- 1 teaspoon ground cumin
- 2 cloves garlic, minced
- 1/4 teaspoon cayenne pepper
- 3/4 cup uncooked white rice
- 3 1/2 cups canned black beans, drained

DIRECTIONS

1. In a stockpot over medium-high heat, heat the oil. Add the onion and garlic and saute for 4 minutes. Add the rice and saute for 2 minutes.

2. Add the vegetable broth, bring to a boil, cover and lower the heat and cook for 20 minutes. Add the spices and black beans.

POLLO FAJITAS

Servings: 5 | Prep: 15m | Cooks: 10m | Total: 55m | Additional: 30m

NUTRITION FACTS

Calories: 210 | Carbohydrates: 5.7g | Fat: 8.3g | Protein: 27.6g | Cholesterol: 113mg

INGREDIENTS

- 1 tablespoon Worcestershire sauce
- 1 1/2 pounds boneless, skinless chicken thighs, cut into strips
- 1 tablespoon cider vinegar
- 1 tablespoon vegetable oil
- 1 tablespoon soy sauce
- 1 onion, thinly sliced
- 1 teaspoon chili powder
- 1 green bell pepper, sliced
- 1 clove garlic, minced
- 1/2 lemon, juiced
- 1 dash hot pepper sauce

DIRECTIONS

1. In a medium bowl, combine Worcestershire sauce, vinegar, soy sauce, chili powder, garlic and hot pepper sauce. Place chicken in sauce, and turn once to coat. Marinate for 30 minutes at room temperature, or cover and refrigerate for several hours.

2. Heat oil in a large skillet over high heat. Add chicken strips to the pan, and saute for 5 minutes. Add the onion and green pepper, and saute another 3 minutes. Remove from heat, and sprinkle with lemon juice.

SIMPLE ROASTED BUTTERNUT SQUASH
Servings: 4 | Prep: 15m | Cooks: 25m | Total: 40m

NUTRITION FACTS

Calories: 177 | Carbohydrates: 30.3g | Fat: 7g | Protein: 2.6g | Cholesterol: 0mg

INGREDIENTS

- 1 butternut squash - peeled, seeded, and cut into 1-inch cubes
- 2 cloves garlic, minced
- 2 tablespoons olive oil
- salt and ground black pepper to taste

DIRECTIONS

1. Preheat oven to 400 degrees F (200 degrees C).
2. Toss butternut squash with olive oil and garlic in a large bowl. Season with salt and black pepper. Arrange coated squash on a baking sheet.
3. Roast in the preheated oven until squash is tender and lightly browned, 25 to 30 minutes.

EASY BAKED TILAPIA
Servings: 4 | Prep: 5m | Cooks: 30m | Total: 35m

NUTRITION FACTS

Calories: 172 | Carbohydrates: 7.3g | Fat: 3.6g | Protein: 24.8g | Cholesterol: 46mg

INGREDIENTS

- 4 (4 ounce) fillets tilapia
- 1/2 teaspoon garlic salt, or to taste
- 2 teaspoons butter
- 1 lemon, sliced
- 1/4 teaspoon Old Bay Seasoning TM, or to taste
- 1 (16 ounce) package frozen cauliflower with broccoli and red pepper

DIRECTIONS

1. Preheat the oven to 375 degrees F (190 degrees F). Grease a 9x13 inch baking dish.
2. Place the tilapia fillets in the bottom of the baking dish and dot with butter. Season with Old Bay seasoning and garlic salt. Top each one with a slice or two of lemon. Arrange the frozen mixed vegetables around the fish, and season lightly with salt and pepper.
3. Cover the dish and bake for 25 to 30 minutes in the preheated oven, until vegetables are tender and fish flakes easily with a fork.

BLACKENED CHICKEN

Servings: 2 | Prep: 10m | Cooks: 10m | Total: 20m

NUTRITION FACTS

Calories: 135 | Carbohydrates: 0.9g | Fat: 3g | Protein: 24.7g | Cholesterol: 67mg

INGREDIENTS

- 1/2 teaspoon paprika
- 1/4 teaspoon dried thyme
- 1/8 teaspoon salt
- 1/8 teaspoon ground white pepper
- 1/4 teaspoon cayenne pepper
- 1/8 teaspoon onion powder
- 1/4 teaspoon ground cumin
- 2 skinless, boneless chicken breast halves

DIRECTIONS

1. Preheat oven to 350 degrees F (175 degrees C). Lightly grease a baking sheet. Heat a cast iron skillet over high heat for 5 minutes until it is smoking hot.
2. Mix together the paprika, salt, cayenne, cumin, thyme, white pepper, and onion powder. Oil the chicken breasts with cooking spray on both sides, then coat the chicken breasts evenly with the spice mixture.
3. Place the chicken in the hot pan, and cook for 1 minute. Turn, and cook 1 minute on other side. Place the breasts on the prepared baking sheet.
4. Bake in the preheated oven until no longer pink in the center and the juices run clear, about 5 minutes.

MEXICAN RICE

Servings: 6 | Prep: 5m | Cooks: 25m | Total: 30m

NUTRITION FACTS

Calories: 158 | Carbohydrates: 29.1g | Fat: 2.8g | Protein: 3.4g | Cholesterol: 1mg

INGREDIENTS

- 1 cup long grain white rice
- 1 tomato, seeded and chopped
- 1 tablespoon vegetable oil
- 1 cube chicken bouillon
- 1 1/2 cups chicken broth
- salt and pepper to taste
- 1/2 onion, finely chopped
- 1/2 teaspoon ground cumin
- 1/2 green bell pepper, finely chopped
- 1/2 cup chopped fresh cilantro
- 1 fresh jalapeno pepper, chopped
- 1 clove garlic, halved

DIRECTIONS

1. In a medium sauce pan, cook rice in oil over medium heat for about 3 minutes. Pour in chicken broth, and bring to a boil. Stir in onion, green pepper, jalapeno, and diced tomato. Season with bouillon cube, salt and pepper, cumin, cilantro, and garlic. Bring to a boil, cover, and reduce heat to low. Cook for 20 minutes.

CHICKEN AND BACON SHISH KABOBS

Servings: 6 | Prep: 25m | Cooks: 20m | Total: 1h45m | Additional: 1h

NUTRITION FACTS

Calories: 235 | Carbohydrates: 14.4g | Fat: 11.4g | Protein: 18.9g | Cholesterol: 47mg

INGREDIENTS

- 1/4 cup soy sauce
- 2 green onions, minced
- 1/4 cup cider vinegar
- 3 skinless, boneless chicken breast halves - cut into chunks
- 2 tablespoons honey
- 1/2 pound sliced thick cut bacon, cut in half
- 2 tablespoons canola oil
- 1 (8 ounce) can pineapple chunks, drained
- 10 large mushrooms, cut in half
- skewers

DIRECTIONS

1. In a large bowl, mix the soy sauce, cider vinegar, honey, canola oil, and green onions. Place the mushrooms and chicken into the mixture, and stir to coat. Cover, and marinate in the refrigerator at least 1 hour.
2. Preheat grill for high heat.
3. Remove the mushrooms and chicken from the marinade and shake off excess. Pour the marinade into a small saucepan and bring to a boil over high heat. Reduce heat to medium-low and simmer for 10 minutes; set aside.
4. Wrap the chicken chunks with bacon, and thread onto skewers so that the bacon is secured. Alternate with mushroom halves and pineapple chunks.
5. Lightly oil the grill grate. Arrange skewers on the prepared grill. Cook 15 to 20 minutes, brushing occasionally with remaining soy sauce mixture, until bacon is crisp and chicken juices run clear.

EMILY'S FAMOUS HASH BROWNS

Servings: 4 | Prep: 20m | Cooks: 15m | Total: 35m

NUTRITION FACTS

Calories: 183 | Carbohydrates: 26.1g | Fat: 6.9g | Protein: 4.7g | Cholesterol: 47mg

INGREDIENTS

- 2 medium russet potatoes, shredded
- 1 egg
- 1/2 medium onion, finely chopped
- 1 cup oil for frying, or as needed
- 1/4 cup all-purpose flour
- salt and pepper to taste

DIRECTIONS

1. Rinse shredded potatoes until water is clear, then drain and squeeze dry. Place shreds in a bowl, and mix in the onion, flour and egg until evenly distributed.
2. Heat about 1/4 inch of oil in a large heavy skillet over medium-high heat. When oil is sizzling hot, place potatoes into the pan in a 1/2 inch thick layer. Cover the whole bottom of the pan, or make separate piles like pancakes. Cook until nicely browned on the bottom, then flip over and brown on the other side. It should take at least 5 minutes per side. If you are cooking them in one big piece, it can be cut into quarters for easier flipping.
3. Remove from pan, and drain on paper towels. Season with salt and pepper and serve immediately.

BROCCOLI BEEF

Servings: 4 | Prep: 15m | Cooks: 15m | Total: 30m

NUTRITION FACTS

Calories: 178 | Carbohydrates: 19g | Fat: 3.2g | Protein: 19.2g | Cholesterol: 39mg

INGREDIENTS

- 1/4 cup all-purpose flour
- 1 pound boneless round steak, cut into bite size pieces
- 1 (10.5 ounce) can beef broth
- 1/4 teaspoon chopped fresh ginger root
- 2 tablespoons white sugar
- 1 clove garlic, minced
- 2 tablespoons soy sauce
- 4 cups chopped fresh broccoli

DIRECTIONS

1. In a small bowl, combine flour, broth, sugar, and soy sauce. Stir until sugar and flour are dissolved.
2. In a large skillet or wok over high heat, cook and stir beef 2 to 4 minutes, or until browned. Stir in broth mixture, ginger, garlic, and broccoli. Bring to a boil, then reduce heat. Simmer 5 to 10 minutes, or until sauce thickens.

KEN'S PERFECT HARD BOILED EGG (AND I MEAN PERFECT)

Servings: 8 | Prep: 5m | Cooks: 20m | Total: 40m | Additional: 15m

NUTRITION FACTS

Calories: 72 | Carbohydrates: 0.4g | Fat: 5g | Protein: 6.3g | Cholesterol: 186mg

INGREDIENTS

- 1 tablespoon salt
- 6 cups water
- 1/4 cup distilled white vinegar
- 8 eggs

DIRECTIONS

1. Combine the salt, vinegar, and water in a large pot, and bring to a boil over high heat. Add the eggs one at a time, being careful not to crack them. Reduce the heat to a gentle boil, and cook for 14 minutes.
2. Once the eggs have cooked, remove them from the hot water, and place into a container of ice water or cold, running water. Cool completely, about 15 minutes. Store in the refrigerator up to 1 week.

SPINACH AND FETA PITA BAKE

Servings: 6 | Prep: 10m | Cooks: 12m | Total: 22m

NUTRITION FACTS

Calories: 350 | Carbohydrates: 41.6g | Fat: 17.1g | Protein: 11.6g | Cholesterol: 13mg

INGREDIENTS

- 1 (6 ounce) tub sun-dried tomato pesto
- 1/2 cup crumbled feta cheese
- 6 (6 inch) whole wheat pita breads
- 2 tablespoons grated Parmesan cheese
- 2 roma (plum) tomatoes, chopped
- 3 tablespoons olive oil
- 1 bunch spinach, rinsed and chopped
- ground black pepper to taste
- 4 fresh mushrooms, sliced

DIRECTIONS

1. Preheat the oven to 350 degrees F (175 degrees C).
2. Spread tomato pesto onto one side of each pita bread and place them pesto-side up on a baking sheet. Top pitas with tomatoes, spinach, mushrooms, feta cheese, and Parmesan cheese; drizzle with olive oil and season with pepper.
3. Bake in the preheated oven until pita breads are crisp, about 12 minutes. Cut pitas into quarters.

PESTO PASTA WITH CHICKEN

Servings: 8 | Prep: 10m | Cooks: 20m | Total: 30m

NUTRITION FACTS

Calories: 328 | Carbohydrates: 43.3g | Fat: 10.1g | Protein: 17.4g | Cholesterol: 22mg

INGREDIENTS

- 1 (16 ounce) package bow tie pasta
- crushed red pepper flakes to taste
- 1 teaspoon olive oil
- 1/3 cup oil-packed sun-dried tomatoes, drained and cut into strips
- 2 cloves garlic, minced
- 1/2 cup pesto sauce
- 2 boneless skinless chicken breasts, cut into bite-size pieces

DIRECTIONS

1. Bring a large pot of lightly salted water to a boil. Add pasta and cook for 8 to 10 minutes or until al dente; drain.
2. Heat oil in a large skillet over medium heat. Saute garlic until tender, then stir in chicken. Season with red pepper flakes. Cook until chicken is golden, and cooked through.
3. In a large bowl, combine pasta, chicken, sun-dried tomatoes and pesto. Toss to coat evenly.

SOUVLAKI

Servings: 12 | Prep: 30m | Cooks: 15m | Total: 2h45m | Additional: 2h

NUTRITION FACTS

Calories: 189 | Carbohydrates: 4.3g | Fat: 8.1g | Protein: 24.2g | Cholesterol: 65mg

INGREDIENTS

- 1 lemon, juiced
- 4 pounds pork tenderloin, cut into 1 inch cubes
- 1/4 cup olive oil
- 2 medium yellow onions, cut into 1 inch pieces
- 1/4 cup soy sauce
- 2 green bell peppers, cut into 1 inch pieces
- 1 teaspoon dried oregano
- skewers
- 3 cloves garlic, crushed

DIRECTIONS

1. In a large glass bowl, mix together lemon juice, olive oil, soy sauce, oregano, and garlic; add pork, onions, and green peppers, and stir to coat. Cover, and refrigerate for 2 to 3 hours.
2. Preheat grill for medium-high heat. Thread pork, peppers, and onions onto skewers.
3. Lightly oil grate. Cook for 10 to 15 minutes, or to desired doneness, turning skewers frequently for even cooking.

ACORN SQUASH

Servings: 2 | Prep: 5m | Cooks: 1m | Total: 1h5m

NUTRITION FACTS

Calories: 189 | Carbohydrates: 35.8g | Fat: 6g | Protein: 1.8g | Cholesterol: 15mg

INGREDIENTS

- 1 medium acorn squash, halved and seeded
- 2 tablespoons brown sugar
- 1 tablespoon butter

DIRECTIONS

1. Preheat oven to 350 degrees F (175 degrees C).
2. Turn acorn squash upside down onto a cookie sheet. Bake in a 350 degrees F (175 degrees C) oven until it begins to soften, approximately 30 to 45 minutes.
3. Remove squash from the oven and turn onto a plate so that the flesh is facing upwards. Place butter and brown sugar into the squash, and place remaining squash over the other piece. Place squash in a baking dish (so the squash won't slide around too much) while baking.
4. Place squash in the 350 degrees F (175 degrees C) oven and bake another 30 minutes.

CHICKEN AND RED WINE SAUCE

Servings: 12 | Prep: 10m | Cooks: 45m | Total: 55m

NUTRITION FACTS

Calories: 214 | Carbohydrates: 19g | Fat: 3.5g | Protein: 22.2g | Cholesterol: 59mg

INGREDIENTS

- 1 tablespoon olive oil
- 1 cup brown sugar
- 1 tablespoon minced garlic
- 1 cup red wine
- 3 pounds skinless, boneless chicken breast halves
- salt and pepper to taste
- 1 tablespoon paprika

DIRECTIONS

1. Heat oil in a large skillet over medium high heat. Cook garlic in oil until tender. Place chicken in the skillet, and cook about 10 minutes on each side, until no longer pink and juices run clear.
2. Drain oil from skillet. Sprinkle chicken with paprika and 1 cup brown sugar. Pour red wine around chicken. Cover, and simmer about 15 to 20 minutes; lightly baste chicken with wine sauce while cooking. Season to taste with salt and pepper.

GREEN BEANS WITH CHERRY TOMATOES

Servings: 6 | Prep: 5m | Cooks: 15m | Total: 20m

NUTRITION FACTS

Calories: 122 | Carbohydrates: 12.6g | Fat: 8g | Protein: 2.6g | Cholesterol: 20mg

INGREDIENTS

- 1 1/2 pounds green beans, trimmed and cut into 2 inch pieces
- 3/4 teaspoon garlic salt
- 1 1/2 cups water
- 3/4 teaspoon pepper
- 1/4 cup butter
- 1 1/2 teaspoons chopped fresh basil
- 1 tablespoon sugar
- 2 cups cherry tomato halves

DIRECTIONS

1. Place beans and water in a large saucepan. Cover, and bring to a boil. Set heat to low, and simmer until tender, about 10 minutes. Drain off water, and set aside.
2. Melt butter in a skillet over medium heat. Stir in sugar, garlic salt, pepper and basil. Add tomatoes, and cook stirring gently just until soft. Pour the tomato mixture over the green beans, and toss gently to blend.

FIERY FISH TACOS WITH CRUNCHY CORN SALSA

Servings: 6 | Prep: 30m | Cooks: 10m | Total: 40m

NUTRITION FACTS

Calories: 351 | Carbohydrates: 40.3g | Fat: 9.6g | Protein: 28.7g | Cholesterol: 43mg

INGREDIENTS

- 2 cups cooked corn kernels

- 1 tablespoon ground black pepper
- 1/2 cup diced red onion
- 2 tablespoons salt, or to taste
- 1 cup peeled, diced jicama
- 6 (4 ounce) fillets tilapia
- 1/2 cup diced red bell pepper
- 2 tablespoons olive oil
- 1 cup fresh cilantro leaves, chopped
- 12 corn tortillas, warmed
- 1 lime, juiced and zested
- 2 tablespoons sour cream, or to taste
- 2 tablespoons cayenne pepper, or to taste

DIRECTIONS

1. Preheat grill for high heat.
2. In a medium bowl, mix together corn, red onion, jicama, red bell pepper, and cilantro. Stir in lime juice and zest.
3. In a small bowl, combine cayenne pepper, ground black pepper, and salt.
4. Brush each fillet with olive oil, and sprinkle with spices to taste.
5. Arrange fillets on grill grate, and cook for 3 minutes per side. For each fiery fish taco, top two corn tortillas with fish, sour cream, and corn salsa.

GARLIC SHRIMP LINGUINE

Servings: 8 | Prep: 10m | Cooks: 20m | Total: 30m

NUTRITION FACTS

Calories: 287 | Carbohydrates: 42.3g | Fat: 4.9g | Protein: 17.6g | Cholesterol: 77mg

INGREDIENTS

- 1 pound uncooked linguine
- 3 cloves garlic, minced
- 1 tablespoon butter
- 1 teaspoon chopped fresh parsley
- 3 tablespoons white wine
- 1 pinch salt and pepper to taste
- 2 teaspoons grated Parmesan cheese
- 1 pound medium shrimp, peeled and deveined

DIRECTIONS

1. Bring a large pot of lightly salted water to a boil. Add pasta and cook for 8 to 10 minutes or until al dente; drain.
2. In a medium saucepan, melt butter over medium low heat; add wine, cheese, garlic, parsley and salt and pepper to taste. Simmer over low heat for 3 to 5 minutes, stirring frequently.
3. Increase heat to medium high and add shrimp to saucepan; cook for about 3 to 4 minutes or until shrimp begins to turn pink. Do not overcook.
4. Divide pasta into portions and spoon sauce on top; garnish with Parmesan cheese and fresh parsley, if desired.

FRIED CABBAGE

Servings: 6 | Prep: 20m | Cooks: 25m | Total: 45m

NUTRITION FACTS

Calories: 47 | Carbohydrates: 5.2g | Fat: 2g | Protein: 2.8g | Cholesterol: 5mg

INGREDIENTS

- 3 slices bacon, chopped
- 1 pinch white sugar
- 1/4 cup chopped onion
- salt and pepper to taste
- 6 cups cabbage, cut into thin wedges
- 1 tablespoon cider vinegar
- 2 tablespoons water

DIRECTIONS

1. Place bacon in a large, deep skillet. Cook over medium-high heat until evenly brown. Remove bacon, and set aside
2. Cook onion in the hot bacon grease until tender. Add cabbage, and stir in water, sugar, salt, and pepper. Cook until cabbage wilts, about 15 minutes. Stir in bacon. Splash with vinegar before serving.

SAUTEED GARLIC ASPARAGUS

Servings: 4 | Prep: 10m | Cooks: 20m | Total: 30m

NUTRITION FACTS

Calories: 102 | Carbohydrates: 5.2g | Fat: 8.8g | Protein: 2.7g | Cholesterol: 23mg

INGREDIENTS

- 3 tablespoons butter or margarine
- 3 cloves garlic, chopped
- 1 bunch fresh asparagus

DIRECTIONS

1. Melt the butter or margarine in a large skillet over medium-high heat. Add the garlic and asparagus spears; cover and cook for 10 minutes, stirring occasionally, or until asparagus is tender. If you like your asparagus well done, reduce heat and cook an additional 10 minutes.

SLOW COOKER CHICKEN CACCIATORE

Servings: 6 | Prep: 15m | Cooks: 9h | Total: 9h15m

NUTRITION FACTS

Calories: 261 | Carbohydrates: 23.7g | Fat: 6.1g | Protein: 27.1g | Cholesterol: 63mg

INGREDIENTS

- 6 skinless, boneless chicken breast halves
- 8 ounces fresh mushrooms, sliced
- 1 (28 ounce) jar spaghetti sauce
- 1 onion, finely diced
- 2 green bell pepper, seeded and cubed
- 2 tablespoons minced garlic

DIRECTIONS

1. Put the chicken in the slow cooker. Top with the spaghetti sauce, green bell peppers, mushrooms, onion, and garlic.
2. Cover, and cook on Low for 7 to 9 hours.

SALSA CHICKEN BURRITO FILLING

Servings: 4 | Prep: 5m | Cooks: 30m | Total: 35m

NUTRITION FACTS

Calories: 107 | Carbohydrates: 9.6g | Fat: 1.5g | Protein: 12.3g | Cholesterol: 30mg

INGREDIENTS

- 2 skinless, boneless chicken breast halves
- 1 teaspoon ground cumin

- 1 (4 ounce) can tomato sauce
- 2 cloves garlic, minced
- 1/4 cup salsa
- 1 teaspoon chili powder
- 1 (1.25 ounce) package taco seasoning mix
- hot sauce to taste

DIRECTIONS

1. Place chicken breasts and tomato sauce in a medium saucepan over medium high heat. Bring to a boil, then add the salsa, seasoning, cumin, garlic and chili powder. Let simmer for 15 minutes.
2. Step 2
3. With a fork, start pulling the chicken meat apart into thin strings. Keep cooking pulled chicken meat and sauce, covered, for another 5 to 10 minutes. Add hot sauce to taste and stir together (Note: You may need to add a bit of water if the mixture is cooked too high and gets too thick.)

GARLIC CHICKEN WITH ORZO NOODLES

Servings: 4 | Prep: 15m | Cooks: 15m | Total: 30m

NUTRITION FACTS

Calories: 351 | Carbohydrates: 40.4g | Fat: 10.6g | Protein: 22.3g | Cholesterol: 38mg

INGREDIENTS

- 1 cup uncooked orzo pasta
- salt to taste
- 2 tablespoons olive oil
- 1 tablespoon chopped fresh parsley
- 2 cloves garlic
- 2 cups fresh spinach leaves
- 1/4 teaspoon crushed red pepper
- grated Parmesan cheese for topping
- 2 skinless, boneless chicken breast halves - cut into bite-size pieces

DIRECTIONS

1. Bring a large pot of lightly salted water to a boil. Add orzo pasta, cook for 8 to 10 minutes, until al dente, and drain.
2. Heat the oil in a skillet over medium-high heat, and cook the garlic and red pepper 1 minute, until garlic is golden brown. Stir in chicken, season with salt, and cook 2 to 5 minutes, until lightly browned and juices run clear. Reduce heat to medium, and mix in the parsley and cooked orzo. Place

spinach in the skillet. Continue cooking 5 minutes, stirring occasionally, until spinach is wilted. Serve topped with Parmesan cheese.

HOMEMADE CRISPY SEASONED FRENCH FRIES
Servings: 8 | Prep: 15m | Cooks: 10m | Total: 25m

NUTRITION FACTS

Calories: 192 | Carbohydrates: 37.8g | Fat: 3.1g | Protein: 3.9g | Cholesterol: 0mg

INGREDIENTS

- 2 1/2 pounds russet potatoes, peeled
- 1 teaspoon salt
- 1 cup all-purpose flour
- 1 teaspoon paprika
- 1 teaspoon garlic salt
- 1/2 cup water, or as needed
- 1 teaspoon onion salt
- 1 cup vegetable oil for frying

DIRECTIONS

1. Slice potatoes into French fries, and place into cold water so they won't turn brown while you prepare the oil.
2. Heat oil in a large skillet over medium-high heat. While the oil is heating, sift the flour, garlic salt, onion salt, (regular) salt, and paprika into a large bowl. Gradually stir in enough water so that the mixture can be drizzled from a spoon.
3. Dip potato slices into the batter one at a time, and place in the hot oil so they are not touching at first. The fries must be placed into the skillet one at a time, or they will clump together. Fry until golden brown and crispy. Remove and drain on paper towels.

GRILLED ASPARAGUS
Servings: 4 | Prep: 15m | Cooks: 3m | Total: 18m

NUTRITION FACTS

Calories: 53 | Carbohydrates: 4.4g | Fat: 3.5g | Protein: 2.5g | Cholesterol: 0mg

INGREDIENTS

- 1 pound fresh asparagus spears, trimmed

- salt and pepper to taste
- 1 tablespoon olive oil

DIRECTIONS

1. Preheat grill for high heat.
2. Lightly coat the asparagus spears with olive oil. Season with salt and pepper to taste.
3. Grill over high heat for 2 to 3 minutes, or to desired tenderness.

PINEAPPLE CHICKEN TENDERS

Servings: 10 | Prep: 30m | Cooks: 1h10m | Total: 45m | Additional: 30m

NUTRITION FACTS

Calories: 160 | Carbohydrates: 14.7g | Fat: 2.2g | Protein: 19.4g | Cholesterol: 52mg

INGREDIENTS

- 1 cup pineapple juice
- 2 pounds chicken breast tenderloins or strips
- 1/2 cup packed brown sugar
- skewers
- 1/3 cup light soy sauce

DIRECTIONS

1. In a small saucepan over medium heat, mix pineapple juice, brown sugar, and soy sauce. Remove from heat just before the mixture comes to a boil.
2. Place chicken tenders in a medium bowl. Cover with the pineapple marinade, and refrigerate for at least 30 minutes.
3. Preheat grill for medium heat. Thread chicken lengthwise onto wooden skewers.
4. Lightly oil the grill grate. Grill chicken tenders 5 minutes per side, or until juices run clear. They cook quickly, so watch them closely.

TURKEY VEGGIE MEATLOAF CUPS

Servings: 10 | Prep: 20m | Cooks: 25m | Total: 50m

NUTRITION FACTS

Calories: 119 | Carbohydrates: 13.6g | Fat: 1g | Protein: 13.2g | Cholesterol: 47mg

INGREDIENTS

- 2 cups coarsely chopped zucchini
- 1 egg
- 1 1/2 cups coarsely chopped onions
- 2 tablespoons Worcestershire sauce
- 1 red bell pepper, coarsely chopped
- 1 tablespoon Dijon mustard
- 1 pound extra lean ground turkey
- 1/2 cup barbecue sauce, or as needed
- 1/2 cup uncooked couscous

DIRECTIONS

1. Preheat oven to 400 degrees F (200 degrees C). Spray 20 muffin cups with cooking spray.
2. Place zucchini, onions, and red bell pepper into a food processor, and pulse several times until finely chopped but not liquefied. Place the vegetables into a bowl, and mix in ground turkey, couscous, egg, Worcestershire sauce, and Dijon mustard until thoroughly combined. Fill each prepared muffin cup about 3/4 full. Top each cup with about 1 teaspoon of barbecue sauce.
3. Bake in the preheated oven until juices run clear, about 25 minutes. Internal temperature of a muffin measured by an instant-read meat thermometer should be at least 160 degrees F (70 degrees C). Let stand 5 minutes before serving.

CANDIED CARROTS

Servings: 4 | Prep: 10m | Cooks: 30m | Total: 40m

NUTRITION FACTS

Calories: 150 | Carbohydrates: 24.5g | Fat: 6g | Protein: 1.2g | Cholesterol: 15mg

INGREDIENTS

- 1 pound carrots, cut into 2 inch pieces
- 1 pinch salt
- 2 tablespoons butter, diced
- 1 pinch ground black pepper
- 1/4 cup packed brown sugar

DIRECTIONS

1. Place carrots in a pot of salted water. Bring water to a boil, reduce heat to a high simmer and cook about 20 to 30 minutes. Do not cook the carrots to a mushy stage!
2. Drain the carrots, reduce the heat to its lowest possible setting and return the carrots to the pan. Stir in butter, brown sugar, salt and pepper. Cook for about 3 to 5 minutes, until sugar is bubbly. Serve hot!

SWEET AND SPICY GREEN BEANS

Servings: 4 | Prep: 15m | Cooks: 10m | Total: 25m

NUTRITION FACTS

Calories: 59 | Carbohydrates: 8.6g | Fat: 2.4g | Protein: 2.1g | Cholesterol: 0mg

INGREDIENTS

- 3/4 pound fresh green beans, trimmed
- 1 teaspoon garlic chili sauce
- 2 tablespoons soy sauce
- 1 teaspoon honey
- 1 clove garlic, minced
- 2 teaspoons canola oil

DIRECTIONS

1. Arrange a steamer basket in a pot over boiling water, and steam the green beans 3 to 4 minutes.
2. In a bowl, mix the soy sauce, garlic, garlic chili sauce, and honey.
3. Heat the canola oil in a skillet over medium heat. Add the green beans, and fry for 3 to 5 minutes. Pour in the soy sauce mixture. Continue cooking and stirring 2 minutes, or until the liquid is nearly evaporated. Serve immediately.

BEST BLACK BEANS

Servings: 4 | Prep: 10m | Cooks: 5m | Total: 15m

NUTRITION FACTS

Calories: 112 | Carbohydrates: 20.8g | Fat: 0.4g | Protein: 7.1g | Cholesterol: 0mg

INGREDIENTS

- 1 (16 ounce) can black beans
- 1 tablespoon chopped fresh cilantro
- 1 small onion, chopped
- 1/4 teaspoon cayenne pepper
- 1 clove garlic, chopped
- salt to taste

DIRECTIONS

1. In a medium saucepan, combine beans, onion, and garlic, and bring to a boil. Reduce heat to medium-low. Season with cilantro, cayenne, and salt. Simmer for 5 minutes, and serve.

HAWAIIAN CHICKEN KABOBS

Servings: 8 | Prep: 10m | Cooks: 20m | Total: 2h30m | Additional: 2h

NUTRITION FACTS

Calories: 203 | Carbohydrates: 17.1g | Fat: 4.2g | Protein: 23.6g | Cholesterol: 61mg

INGREDIENTS

- 3 tablespoons soy sauce
- 1/4 teaspoon garlic powder
- 3 tablespoons brown sugar
- 8 skinless, boneless chicken breast halves - cut into 2 inch pieces
- 2 tablespoons sherry
- 1 (20 ounce) can pineapple chunks, drained
- 1 tablespoon sesame oil
- skewers
- 1/4 teaspoon ground ginger

DIRECTIONS

1. In a shallow glass dish, mix the soy sauce, brown sugar, sherry, sesame oil, ginger, and garlic powder. Stir the chicken pieces and pineapple into the marinade until well coated. Cover, and marinate in the refrigerator at least 2 hours.
2. Preheat grill to medium-high heat.
3. Lightly oil the grill grate. Thread chicken and pineapple alternately onto skewers. Grill 15 to 20 minutes, turning occasionally, or until chicken juices run clear.

QUICK BAKED ZUCCHINI CHIPS

Servings: 4 | Prep: 5m | Cooks: 10m | Total: 15m

NUTRITION FACTS

Calories: 92 | Carbohydrates: 13.8g | Fat: 1.7g | Protein: 6.1g | Cholesterol: 2mg

INGREDIENTS

- 2 medium zucchini, cut into 1/4-inch slices
- 2 tablespoons grated Parmesan cheese

- 1/2 cup seasoned dry bread crumbs
- 2 egg whites
- 1/8 teaspoon ground black pepper

DIRECTIONS

1. Preheat the oven to 475 degrees F (245 degrees C).
2. In one small bowl, stir together the bread crumbs, pepper and Parmesan cheese. Place the egg whites in a separate bowl. Dip zucchini slices into the egg whites, then coat the breadcrumb mixture. Place on a greased baking sheet.
3. Bake for 5 minutes in the preheated oven, then turn over and bake for another 5 to 10 minutes, until browned and crispy.

SLOW COOKER SPICY BLACK-EYED PEAS

Servings: 10 | Prep: 30m | Cooks: 6h | Total: 6h30m

NUTRITION FACTS

Calories: 199 | Carbohydrates: 30.2g | Fat: 2.9g | Protein: 14.1g | Cholesterol: 10mg

INGREDIENTS

- 6 cups water
- 8 ounces diced ham
- 1 cube chicken bouillon
- 4 slices bacon, chopped
- 1 pound dried black-eyed peas, sorted and rinsed
- 1/2 teaspoon cayenne pepper
- 1 onion, diced
- 1 1/2 teaspoons cumin
- 2 cloves garlic, diced
- salt, to taste
- 1 red bell pepper, stemmed, seeded, and diced
- 1 teaspoon ground black pepper
- 1 jalapeno chile, seeded and minced

DIRECTIONS

1. Pour the water into a slow cooker, add the bouillon cube, and stir to dissolve. Combine the black-eyed peas, onion, garlic, bell pepper, jalapeno pepper, ham, bacon, cayenne pepper, cumin, salt, and pepper; stir to blend. Cover the slow cooker and cook on Low for 6 to 8 hours until the beans are tender.

ROASTED BEETS 'N' SWEETS

Servings: 6 | Prep: 15m | Cooks: 1h | Total: 1h15m

NUTRITION FACTS

Calories: 198 | Carbohydrates: 34.3g | Fat: 5.9g | Protein: 3.5g | Cholesterol: 0mg

INGREDIENTS

- 6 medium beets, peeled and cut into chunks
- 1 teaspoon ground black pepper
- 2 1/2 tablespoons olive oil, divided
- 1 teaspoon sugar
- 1 teaspoon garlic powder
- 3 medium sweet potatoes, cut into chunks
- 1 teaspoon kosher salt
- 1 large sweet onion, chopped

DIRECTIONS

1. Preheat oven to 400 degrees F (200 degrees C).
2. In a bowl, toss the beets with 1/2 tablespoon olive oil to coat. Spread in a single layer on a baking sheet.
3. Mix the remaining 2 tablespoons olive oil, garlic powder, salt, pepper, and sugar in a large resealable plastic bag. Place the sweet potatoes and onion in the bag. Seal bag, and shake to coat vegetables with the oil mixture.
4. Bake beets 15 minutes in the preheated oven. Mix sweet potato mixture with the beets on the baking sheet. Continue baking 45 minutes, stirring after 20 minutes, until all vegetables are tender.

FRESH TOMATO SALSA

Servings: 4 | Prep: 10m | Cooks: 1h | Total: 1h10m | Additional: 1h

NUTRITION FACTS

Calories: 51 | Carbohydrates: 9.7g | Fat: 0.2g | Protein: 2.1g | Cholesterol: 0mg

INGREDIENTS

- 3 tomatoes, chopped
- 1/2 cup chopped fresh cilantro
- 1/2 cup finely diced onion
- 1 teaspoon salt
- 5 serrano chiles, finely chopped

- 2 teaspoons lime juice

DIRECTIONS

1. In a medium bowl, stir together tomatoes, onion, chili peppers, cilantro, salt, and lime juice. Chill for one hour in the refrigerator before serving.

QUICK BAKED ZUCCHINI CHIPS

Servings: 4 | Prep: 5m | Cooks: 10m | Total: 15m

NUTRITION FACTS

Calories: 92 | Carbohydrates: 13.8g | Fat: 1.7g | Protein: 6.1g | Cholesterol: 2mg

INGREDIENTS

- 2 medium zucchini, cut into 1/4-inch slices
- 2 tablespoons grated Parmesan cheese
- 1/2 cup seasoned dry bread crumbs
- 2 egg whites
- 1/8 teaspoon ground black pepper

DIRECTIONS

1. Preheat the oven to 475 degrees F (245 degrees C).
2. In one small bowl, stir together the bread crumbs, pepper and Parmesan cheese. Place the egg whites in a separate bowl. Dip zucchini slices into the egg whites, then coat the breadcrumb mixture. Place on a greased baking sheet.
3. Bake for 5 minutes in the preheated oven, then turn over and bake for another 5 to 10 minutes, until browned and crispy.

SPICED SWEET ROASTED RED PEPPER HUMMUS

Servings: 8 | Prep: 15m | Cooks: 1h | Total: 1h15m | Additional: 1h

NUTRITION FACTS

Calories: 64 | Carbohydrates: 9.6g | Fat: 2.2g | Protein: 2.5g | Cholesterol: 0mg

INGREDIENTS

- 1 (15 ounce) can garbanzo beans, drained
- 1/2 teaspoon ground cumin
- 1 (4 ounce) jar roasted red peppers

- 1/2 teaspoon cayenne pepper
- 3 tablespoons lemon juice
- 1/4 teaspoon salt
- 1 1/2 tablespoons tahini
- 1 tablespoon chopped fresh parsley
- 1 clove garlic, minced

DIRECTIONS

1. In an electric blender or food processor, puree the chickpeas, red peppers, lemon juice, tahini, garlic, cumin, cayenne, and salt. Process, using long pulses, until the mixture is fairly smooth, and slightly fluffy. Make sure to scrape the mixture off the sides of the food processor or blender in between pulses. Transfer to a serving bowl and refrigerate for at least 1 hour. (The hummus can be made up to 3 days ahead and refrigerated. Return to room temperature before serving.)
2. Sprinkle the hummus with the chopped parsley before serving.

MAPLE DILL CARROTS

Servings: 4 | Prep: 10m | Cooks: 10m | Total: 20m

NUTRITION FACTS

Calories: 117 | Carbohydrates: 16.1g | Fat: 6g | Protein: 1g | Cholesterol: 15mg

INGREDIENTS

- 3 cups peeled and sliced carrots
- 1 1/2 tablespoons chopped fresh dill
- 2 tablespoons butter
- 1/2 teaspoon salt
- 2 tablespoons brown sugar
- 1/2 teaspoon black pepper

DIRECTIONS

1. Place carrots in a skillet and pour in just enough water to cover. Bring to a boil over medium heat; simmer until water has evaporated and the carrots are tender. Stir in butter, brown sugar, dill, salt, and pepper.

BAKED SOY LEMON CHOPS

Servings: 4 | Prep: 15m | Cooks: 40m | Total: 1h50m | Additional: 55m

NUTRITION FACTS

Calories: 193 | Carbohydrates: 5.1g | Fat: 6.7g | Protein: 27.1g | Cholesterol: 65mg

INGREDIENTS

- 1/2 cup soy sauce
- 1/2 teaspoon ground black pepper
- 1 tablespoon Worcestershire sauce
- 1 teaspoon vegetable oil
- 4 cloves garlic, minced
- 4 pork chops
- 2 tablespoons lemon juice

DIRECTIONS

1. In a shallow dish, combine soy sauce, Worcestershire sauce, garlic, lemon juice, pepper and oil. Add pork chops, and turn to coat evenly. Cover, and refrigerate for at least 1 hour.
2. Preheat oven to 375 degrees F (190 degrees C).
3. Place marinated pork chops in a roasting pan, and bake in preheated oven for 35 to 40 minutes, basting meat often with marinade.

VIETNAMESE FRESH SPRING ROLLS
Servings: 8 | Prep: 45m | Cooks: 5m | Total: 50m

NUTRITION FACTS

Calories: 82 | Carbohydrates: 15.8g | Fat: 0.7g | Protein: 3.3g | Cholesterol: 11mg

INGREDIENTS

- 2 ounces rice vermicelli
- 1/4 cup water
- 8 rice wrappers (8.5 inch diameter)
- 2 tablespoons fresh lime juice
- 8 large cooked shrimp - peeled, deveined and cut in half
- 1 clove garlic, minced
- 1 1/3 tablespoons chopped fresh Thai basil
- 2 tablespoons white sugar
- 3 tablespoons chopped fresh mint leaves
- 1/2 teaspoon garlic chili sauce
- 3 tablespoons chopped fresh cilantro
- 3 tablespoons hoisin sauce

- 2 leaves lettuce, chopped
- 1 teaspoon finely chopped peanuts
- 4 teaspoons fish sauce

DIRECTIONS

1. Bring a medium saucepan of water to boil. Boil rice vermicelli 3 to 5 minutes, or until al dente, and drain.
2. Fill a large bowl with warm water. Dip one wrapper into the hot water for 1 second to soften. Lay wrapper flat. In a row across the center, place 2 shrimp halves, a handful of vermicelli, basil, mint, cilantro and lettuce, leaving about 2 inches uncovered on each side. Fold uncovered sides inward, then tightly roll the wrapper, beginning at the end with the lettuce. Repeat with remaining ingredients.
3. In a small bowl, mix the fish sauce, water, lime juice, garlic, sugar and chili sauce.
4. In another small bowl, mix the hoisin sauce and peanuts.
5. Serve rolled spring rolls with the fish sauce and hoisin sauce mixtures.

GREEN BEAN AND MUSHROOM MEDLEY

Servings: 6 | Prep: 20m | Cooks: 15m | Total: 35m

NUTRITION FACTS

Calories: 103 | Carbohydrates: 7.7g | Fat: 7.9g | Protein: 1.9g | Cholesterol: 20mg

INGREDIENTS

- 1/2 pound fresh green beans, cut into 1-inch lengths
- 1 teaspoon salt
- 2 carrots, cut into thick strips
- 1/2 teaspoon seasoned salt
- 1/4 cup butter
- 1/4 teaspoon garlic salt
- 1 onion, sliced
- 1/4 teaspoon white pepper
- 1/2 pound fresh mushrooms, sliced

DIRECTIONS

1. Place green beans and carrots in 1 inch of boiling water. Cover, and cook until tender but still firm. Drain.

2. Melt butter in a large skillet over medium heat. Saute onions and mushrooms until almost tender. Reduce heat, cover, and simmer 3 minutes. Stir in green beans, carrots, salt, seasoned salt, garlic salt, and white pepper. Cover, and cook for 5 minutes over medium heat.

HONEYED PORK CHOPS

Servings: 6 | Prep: 15m | Cooks: 1h10m | Total: 1h25m

NUTRITION FACTS

Calories: 239 | Carbohydrates: 10.6g | Fat: 10.1g | Protein: 25.8g | Cholesterol: 0mg

INGREDIENTS

- 2 tablespoons vegetable oil
- 1/4 cup soy sauce
- 6 boneless pork chops
- 1 small onion, chopped
- 3 tablespoons honey
- 1/4 teaspoon ground ginger
- 1/2 cup water
- 1/8 teaspoon ground black pepper

DIRECTIONS

1. Preheat oven to 325 degrees F (165 degrees C).
2. Heat the oil in a skillet over medium heat, and brown the pork chops about 5 minutes on each side. Transfer to a baking dish.
3. In a bowl, mix the honey, water, soy sauce, onion, ginger, and pepper. Pour over the pork chops in the baking dish.
4. Bake pork chops 1 hour in the preheated oven, to an internal temperature of 145 degrees F (63 degrees C).

CHICKPEA CURRY

Servings: 8 | Prep: 10m | Cooks: 30m | Total: 40m

NUTRITION FACTS

Calories: 135 | Carbohydrates: 20.5g | Fat: 4.5g | Protein: 4.1g | Cholesterol: 0mg

INGREDIENTS

- 2 tablespoons vegetable oil

- 1 teaspoon ground coriander
- 2 onions, minced
- salt
- 2 cloves garlic, minced
- 1 teaspoon cayenne pepper
- 2 teaspoons fresh ginger root, finely chopped
- 1 teaspoon ground turmeric
- 6 whole cloves
- 2 (15 ounce) cans garbanzo beans
- 2 (2 inch) sticks cinnamon, crushed
- 1 cup chopped fresh cilantro
- 1 teaspoon ground cumin

DIRECTIONS

1. Heat oil in a large frying pan over medium heat, and fry onions until tender.
2. Stir in garlic, ginger, cloves, cinnamon, cumin, coriander, salt, cayenne, and turmeric. Cook for 1 minute over medium heat, stirring constantly. Mix in garbanzo beans and their liquid. Continue to cook and stir until all ingredients are well blended and heated through. Remove from heat. Stir in cilantro just before serving, reserving 1 tablespoon for garnish.

GINGER VEGGIE STIR-FRY

Servings: 6 | Prep: 25m | Cooks: 15m | Total: 40m

NUTRITION FACTS

Calories: 119 | Carbohydrates: 8g | Fat: 9.3g | Protein: 2.2g | Cholesterol: 0mg

INGREDIENTS

- 1 tablespoon cornstarch
- 3/4 cup julienned carrots
- 1 1/2 cloves garlic, crushed
- 1/2 cup halved green beans
- 2 teaspoons chopped fresh ginger root, divided
- 2 tablespoons soy sauce
- 1/4 cup vegetable oil, divided
- 2 1/2 tablespoons water
- 1 small head broccoli, cut into florets
- 1/4 cup chopped onion
- 1/2 cup snow peas
- 1/2 tablespoon salt

DIRECTIONS

1. In a large bowl, blend cornstarch, garlic, 1 teaspoon ginger, and 2 tablespoons vegetable oil until cornstarch is dissolved. Mix in broccoli, snow peas, carrots, and green beans, tossing to lightly coat.
2. Heat remaining 2 tablespoons oil in a large skillet or wok over medium heat. Cook vegetables in oil for 2 minutes, stirring constantly to prevent burning. Stir in soy sauce and water. Mix in onion, salt, and remaining 1 teaspoon ginger. Cook until vegetables are tender but still crisp.

SPICY CHICKEN BREASTS

Servings: 4 | Prep: 15m | Cooks: 15m | Total: 30m

NUTRITION FACTS

Calories: 173 | Carbohydrates: 9.2g | Fat: 2.4g | Protein: 29.2g | Cholesterol: 68mg

INGREDIENTS

- 2 1/2 tablespoons paprika
- 1 tablespoon dried thyme
- 2 tablespoons garlic powder
- 1 tablespoon ground cayenne pepper
- 1 tablespoon salt
- 1 tablespoon ground black pepper
- 1 tablespoon onion powder
- 4 skinless, boneless chicken breast halves

DIRECTIONS

1. In a medium bowl, mix together the paprika, garlic powder, salt, onion powder, thyme, cayenne pepper, and ground black pepper. Set aside about 3 tablespoons of this seasoning mixture for the chicken; store the remainder in an airtight container for later use (for seasoning fish, meats, or vegetables).
2. Preheat grill for medium-high heat. Rub some of the reserved 3 tablespoons of seasoning onto both sides of the chicken breasts.
3. Lightly oil the grill grate. Place chicken on the grill, and cook for 6 to 8 minutes on each side, until juices run clear.

EASY SLOW COOKER MEATBALLS

Servings: 16 | Prep: 20m | Cooks: 8h | Total: 8h20m

NUTRITION FACTS

INGREDIENTS

- 1 1/2 pounds ground beef
- 1 egg, beaten
- 1 1/4 cups Italian seasoned bread crumbs
- 1 (28 ounce) jar spaghetti sauce
- 1/4 cup chopped fresh parsley
- 1 (16 ounce) can crushed tomatoes
- 2 cloves garlic, minced
- 1 (14.25 ounce) can tomato puree
- 1 medium yellow onion, chopped

DIRECTIONS

1. In a bowl, mix the ground beef, bread crumbs, parsley, garlic, onion, and egg. Shape the mixture into 16 meatballs.
2. In a slow cooker, mix the spaghetti sauce, crushed tomatoes, and tomato puree. Place the meatballs into the sauce mixture. Cook on Low for 6 to 8 hours.

MAPLE-GARLIC MARINATED PORK TENDERLOIN

Servings: 6 | Prep: 5m | Cooks: 25m | Total: 8h30m | Additional: 8h

NUTRITION FACTS

Calories: 288 | Carbohydrates: 36.8g | Fat: 4.9g | Protein: 23.5g | Cholesterol: 74mg

INGREDIENTS

- 2 tablespoons Dijon mustard
- fresh ground black pepper to taste
- 1 teaspoon sesame oil
- 1 cup maple syrup
- 3 cloves garlic, minced
- 1 1/2 pounds pork tenderloin

DIRECTIONS

1. Combine mustard, sesame oil, garlic, pepper, and maple syrup. Place pork in a shallow dish and coat thoroughly with marinade. Cover, then chill in the refrigerator at least eight hours, or overnight.
2. Preheat grill for medium-low heat.

3. Remove pork from marinade, and set aside. Transfer remaining marinade to a small saucepan, and cook on the stove over medium-low heat for 5 minutes.

4. Brush grate with oil, and place meat on grate. Grill pork, basting with reserved marinade, for approximately 15 to 25 minutes, or until interior is no longer pink. Avoid using high temperatures as marinade will burn.

SESAME GREEN BEANS

Servings: 4 | Prep: 5m | Cooks: 25m | Total: 30m

NUTRITION FACTS

Calories: 78 | Carbohydrates: 8.6g | Fat: 4.6g | Protein: 2.5g | Cholesterol: 0mg

INGREDIENTS

- 1 tablespoon olive oil
- 1/4 cup chicken broth
- 1 tablespoon sesame seeds
- 1/4 teaspoon salt
- 1 pound fresh green beans, cut into 2 inch pieces
- freshly ground black pepper to taste

DIRECTIONS

1. Heat oil in a large skillet or wok over medium heat. Add sesame seeds. When seeds start to darken, stir in green beans. Cook, stirring, until the beans turn bright green.

2. Pour in chicken broth, salt and pepper. Cover and cook until beans are tender-crisp, about 10 minutes. Uncover and cook until liquid evaporates.

CHICKEN WITH GARLIC, BASIL, AND PARSLEY

Servings: 4 | Prep: 10m | Cooks: 40m | Total: 50m

NUTRITION FACTS

Calories: 150 | Carbohydrates: 4.1g | Fat: 3.1g | Protein: 25.6g | Cholesterol: 67mg

INGREDIENTS

- 1 tablespoon dried parsley, divided
- 1/2 teaspoon salt
- 1 tablespoon dried basil, divided
- 1/2 teaspoon crushed red pepper flakes

- 4 skinless, boneless chicken breast halves
- 2 tomatoes, sliced
- 4 cloves garlic, thinly sliced

DIRECTIONS

1. Preheat oven to 350 degrees F (175 degrees C). Coat a 9x13 inch baking dish with cooking spray.
2. Sprinkle 1 teaspoon parsley and 1 teaspoon basil evenly over the bottom of the baking dish. Arrange chicken breast halves in the dish, and sprinkle evenly with garlic slices. In a small bowl, mix the remaining 2 teaspoons parsley, remaining 2 teaspoons basil, salt, and red pepper; sprinkle over the chicken. Top with tomato slices.
3. Bake covered in the preheated oven 25 minutes. Remove cover, and continue baking 15 minutes, or until chicken juices run clear.

SOUTHERN FRIED CABBAGE

Servings: 6 | Prep: 5m | Cooks: 10m | Total: 15m

NUTRITION FACTS

Calories: 189 | Carbohydrates: 13.6g | Fat: 14.2g | Protein: 4.4g | Cholesterol: 5mg

INGREDIENTS

- 3 slices bacon, cut into thirds
- 1 head cabbage, cored and sliced
- 1/3 cup vegetable oil
- 1 white onion, chopped
- 1 teaspoon salt, or to taste
- 1 pinch white sugar
- 1 teaspoon ground black pepper, or to taste

DIRECTIONS

1. Place the bacon and vegetable oil into a large pot over medium heat. Season with salt and pepper. Cook for about 5 minutes, or until bacon is crisp. Add cabbage, onion, and sugar to the pot; cook and stir continuously for 5 minutes, until tender.

CHICKEN SATAY

Servings: 12 | Prep: 2h10m | Cooks: 20m | Total: 2h40m | Additional: 10m

NUTRITION FACTS

Calories: 162 | Carbohydrates: 4.1g | Fat: 3g | Protein: 28.8g | Cholesterol: 68mg

INGREDIENTS

- 2 tablespoons creamy peanut butter
- 2 tablespoons curry powder
- 1/2 cup soy sauce
- 2 cloves garlic, chopped
- 1/2 cup lemon or lime juice
- 1 teaspoon hot pepper sauce
- 1 tablespoon brown sugar
- 6 skinless, boneless chicken breast halves - cubed

DIRECTIONS

1. In a mixing bowl, combine peanut butter, soy sauce, lime juice, brown sugar, curry powder, garlic and hot pepper sauce. Place the chicken breasts in the marinade and refrigerate. Let the chicken marinate at least 2 hours, overnight is best.
2. Preheat a grill to high heat.
3. Weave the chicken onto skewers, then grill for 5 minutes per side.

HONEY ORANGE GREEN BEANS

Servings: 4 | Prep: 15m | Cooks: 25m | Total: 40m

NUTRITION FACTS

Calories: 340 | Carbohydrates: 52g | Fat: 8.9g | Protein: 14.7g | Cholesterol: 4mg

INGREDIENTS

- 1 cup vegetable broth
- 1/4 teaspoon crushed red pepper flakes
- 12 dehydrated sun-dried tomatoes
- 1 clove garlic, minced
- 1 (8 ounce) package uncooked penne pasta
- 1 bunch fresh spinach, rinsed and torn into bite-size pieces
- 2 tablespoons pine nuts
- 1/4 cup grated Parmesan cheese
- 1 tablespoon olive oil

DIRECTIONS

1. In a small saucepan, bring the broth to a boil. Remove from heat. Place the sun-dried tomatoes in the broth 15 minutes, or until softened. Drain, reserving broth, and coarsely chop.
2. Bring a large pot of lightly salted water to a boil. Place penne pasta in the pot, cook 9 to 12 minutes, until al dente, and drain.
3. Place the pine nuts in a skillet over medium heat. Cook and stir until lightly toasted.
4. Heat the olive oil and red pepper flakes in a skillet over medium heat, and saute the garlic 1 minute, until tender. Mix in the spinach, and cook until almost wilted. Pour in the reserved broth, and stir in the chopped sun-dried tomatoes. Continue cooking 2 minutes, or until heated through.
5. In a large bowl, toss the cooked pasta with the spinach and tomato mixture and pine nuts. Serve with Parmesan cheese.

SMOTHERED GREEN BEANS

Servings: 6 | Prep: 20m | Cooks: 30m | Total: 50m

NUTRITION FACTS

Calories: 97 | Carbohydrates: 7g | Fat: 5.4g | Protein: 6.2g | Cholesterol: 14mg

INGREDIENTS

- 6 thick slices bacon, chopped
- 1 cup water
- 1/2 cup onions, minced
- 1/8 teaspoon salt
- 1 teaspoon minced garlic
- 1 pinch ground black pepper
- 1 pound fresh green beans, trimmed

DIRECTIONS

1. Place bacon in a large, deep skillet. Cook over medium high heat until the fat begins to render. Stir in onions and garlic; let cook for 1 minute. Stir in beans and water. Let the beans cook until the water has evaporated and the beans are tender. If the beans are not tender once the water has evaporated, add a small amount more water and let them cook until tender. Season with salt and pepper (to taste) and serve.

SPICY BAKED SWEET POTATO FRIES

Servings: 6 | Prep: 10m | Cooks: 1h | Total: 1h10m

NUTRITION FACTS

Calories: 169 | Carbohydrates: 29.2g | Fat: 4.7g | Protein: 2.1g | Cholesterol: 0mg

INGREDIENTS

- 6 sweet potatoes, cut into French fries
- 3 tablespoons taco seasoning mix
- 2 tablespoons canola oil
- 1/4 teaspoon cayenne pepper

DIRECTIONS

1. Preheat the oven to 425 degrees F (220 degrees C).
2. In a plastic bag, combine the sweet potatoes, canola oil, taco seasoning, and cayenne pepper. Close and shake the bag until the fries are evenly coated. Spread the fries out in a single layer on two large baking sheets.
3. Bake for 30 minutes, or until crispy and brown on one side. Turn the fries over using a spatula, and cook for another 30 minutes, or until they are all crispy on the outside and tender inside. Thinner fries may not take as long.

BAKED SWEET POTATO STICKS

Servings: 8 | Prep: 15m | Cooks: 40m | Total: 55m

NUTRITION FACTS

Calories: 132 | Carbohydrates: 27g | Fat: 1.9g | Protein: 2.6g | Cholesterol: 0mg

INGREDIENTS

- 1 tablespoon olive oil
- 8 sweet potatoes, sliced lengthwise into quarters
- 1/2 teaspoon paprika

DIRECTIONS

1. Preheat oven to 400 degrees F (200 degrees C). Lightly grease a baking sheet
2. In a large bowl, mix olive oil and paprika. Add potato sticks, and stir by hand to coat. Place on the prepared baking sheet.
3. Bake 40 minutes in the preheated oven.

COWBOY MASHED POTATOES

Servings: 10 | Prep: 20m | Cooks: 20m | Total: 40m

NUTRITION FACTS

Calories: 175 | Carbohydrates: 24.6g | Fat: 7.3g | Protein: 4.7g | Cholesterol: 0mg

INGREDIENTS

- 1 pound red potatoes
- 1 (10 ounce) package frozen white corn, thawed
- 1 pound Yukon Gold (yellow) potatoes
- 1/4 cup butter
- 1 fresh jalapeno pepper, sliced
- 1/2 cup shredded Cheddar cheese
- 12 ounces baby carrots
- salt and pepper to taste
- 4 cloves garlic

DIRECTIONS

1. Place red potatoes, yellow potatoes, jalapeno pepper, carrots and garlic cloves in a large pot. Cover with water, and bring to a boil over high heat. Cook 15 to 20 minutes, or until potatoes are tender. Drain water from pot.
2. Stir in corn and butter. Mash the mixture with a potato masher until butter is melted and potatoes have reached desired consistency. Mix in cheese, salt, and pepper. Serve hot.

BALSAMIC CHICKEN

Servings: 4 | Prep: 5m | Cooks: 20m | Total: 45m | Additional: 20m

NUTRITION FACTS

Calories: 194 | Carbohydrates: 9.8g | Fat: 4.9g | Protein: 26.4g | Cholesterol: 66mg

INGREDIENTS

- 1/3 cup balsamic vinegar
- 1 teaspoon dried Italian herb seasoning
- 1/2 cup chicken broth
- 4 skinless, boneless chicken breast halves
- 2 tablespoons white sugar
- 1 tablespoon olive oil
- 1 clove garlic, minced

DIRECTIONS

1. Whisk together the balsamic vinegar, chicken broth, sugar, garlic, and Italian seasoning in a bowl, place the chicken breasts in the marinade, and marinate for 10 minutes on each side.

2. Heat the olive oil in a large skillet over medium-high heat. Remove the chicken from the marinade and reserve the marinade. Place the chicken in the heated pan and cook until they start to brown and are no longer pink inside, about 7 minutes per side. Pour the marinade into the skillet, and cook until it thickens slightly, turning the chicken breasts over once or twice, about 5 minutes.

COD WITH ITALIAN CRUMB TOPPING

Servings: 4 | Prep: 15m | Cooks: 10m | Total: 25m

NUTRITION FACTS

Calories: 131 | Carbohydrates: 7g | Fat: 2.9g | Protein: 18.1g | Cholesterol: 39mg

INGREDIENTS

- 1/4 cup fine dry bread crumbs
- 1/8 teaspoon garlic powder
- 2 tablespoons grated Parmesan cheese
- 1/8 teaspoon ground black pepper
- 1 tablespoon cornmeal
- 4 (3 ounce) fillets cod fillets
- 1 teaspoon olive oil
- 1 egg white, lightly beaten
- 1/2 teaspoon Italian seasoning

DIRECTIONS

1. Preheat oven to 450 degrees F (230 degrees C).
2. In a small shallow bowl, stir together the bread crumbs, cheese, cornmeal, oil, italian seasoning, garlic powder and pepper; set aside.
3. Coat the rack of a broiling pan with cooking spray. Place the cod on the rack, folding under any thin edges of the filets. Brush with the egg white, then spoon the crumb mixture evenly on top.
4. Bake in a preheated oven for 10 to 12 minutes or until the fish flakes easily when tested with a fork and is opaque all the way through.

SIMPLE BAKED APPLES

Servings: 12 | Prep: 30m | Cooks: 1h | Total: 1h30m

NUTRITION FACTS

Calories: 136 | Carbohydrates: 26.1g | Fat: 3.8g | Protein: 1.7g | Cholesterol: 1mg

INGREDIENTS

- 6 apples - peeled, cored and sliced
- 1/4 teaspoon ground cloves
- 1/2 cup white sugar
- 1/2 cup raisins
- 3 tablespoons all-purpose flour
- 1/2 cup chopped walnuts
- 1/2 teaspoon ground cinnamon
- 1/2 cup whole milk
- 1/2 teaspoon ground nutmeg

DIRECTIONS

1. Preheat oven to 350 degrees F (175 degrees C). Grease a 2 quart casserole dish, or coat with non-stick cooking spray.
2. Place apples in a large bowl. In a small bowl, mix together sugar, flour, cinnamon, nutmeg and cloves. Stir spice mixture into apples until evenly distributed. Fold in raisins and walnuts. Spoon into prepared dish. Pour milk evenly over apple mixture.
3. Bake in preheated oven for 45 to 60 minutes, or until soft and bubbly. Allow to cool slightly before serving.

ASPARAGUS WITH PARMESAN CRUST

Servings: 4 | Prep: 10m | Cooks: 15m | Total: 25m

NUTRITION FACTS

Calories: 93 | Carbohydrates: 7g | Fat: 5.6g | Protein: 5.3g | Cholesterol: 6mg

INGREDIENTS

- 1 pound thin asparagus spears
- freshly ground black pepper to taste
- 1 tablespoon extra virgin olive oil
- 1/4 cup balsamic vinegar, or to taste
- 1 ounce shaved Parmesan cheese

DIRECTIONS

1. Preheat oven to 450 degrees F (230 degrees C).
2. Place asparagus on a baking sheet. Drizzle with olive oil, and toss to coat. Arrange asparagus spears in a single layer. Spread Parmesan cheese over asparagus, and season with freshly ground black pepper.
3. Bake 12 to 15 minutes in the preheated oven, until cheese is melted and asparagus is tender but crisp. Serve immediately on warm plates, sprinkling with balsamic vinegar to taste.

CHICKEN IN A POT

Servings: 4 | Prep: 20m | Cooks: 20m | Total: 40m

NUTRITION FACTS

Calories: 206 | Carbohydrates: 6.9g | Fat: 6.6g | Protein: 28.7g | Cholesterol: 73mg

INGREDIENTS

- 3/4 cup chicken broth
- 1 clove garlic, minced
- 1 1/2 tablespoons tomato paste
- 4 boneless, skinless chicken breast halves
- 1/4 teaspoon ground black pepper
- 3 tablespoons dry bread crumbs
- 1/2 teaspoon dried oregano
- 2 teaspoons olive oil
- 1/8 teaspoon salt
- 2 cups fresh sliced mushrooms

DIRECTIONS

1. In a medium bowl, combine the broth, tomato paste, ground black pepper, oregano, salt and garlic. Mix well and set aside.
2. Dredge the chicken in the bread crumbs, coating well. Heat the oil in a large skillet over medium high heat. Saute the chicken in the oil for 2 minutes per side, or until lightly browned.
3. Add the reserved broth mixture and the mushrooms to the skillet and bring to a boil. Then cover, reduce heat to low and simmer for 20 minutes. Remove chicken and set aside, covering to keep it warm.
4. Bring broth mixture to a boil and cook for 4 minutes, or until reduced to desired thickness. Spoon sauce over the chicken and serve.

JAPANESE ZUCCHINI AND ONIONS

Servings: 4 | Prep: 10m | Cooks: 10m | Total: 20m

NUTRITION FACTS

Calories: 110 | Carbohydrates: 8.1g | Fat: 8.2g | Protein: 2.7g | Cholesterol: 0mg

INGREDIENTS

- 2 tablespoons vegetable oil
- 1 tablespoon soy sauce

- 1 medium onion, thinly sliced
- 1 tablespoon toasted sesame seeds
- 2 medium zucchinis, cut into thin strips
- ground black pepper
- 2 tablespoons teriyaki sauce

DIRECTIONS

1. Warm the oil in a large skillet over medium heat. Stir in onions, and cook 5 minutes. Add zucchini, and cook, stirring, about 1 minute. Stir in teriyaki sauce, soy sauce, and sesame seeds. Cook until zucchini are tender, about 5 minutes. Stir in ground pepper, and serve immediately.

CHICKEN WITH ASPARAGUS AND ROASTED RED PEPPERS

Servings: 4 | Prep: 15m | Cooks: 25m | Total: 40m

NUTRITION FACTS

Calories: 184 | Carbohydrates: 6.5g | Fat: 5g | Protein: 17.6g | Cholesterol: 68mg

INGREDIENTS

- 1/2 cup chicken broth
- 1 clove garlic, minced
- 1 pound boned and skinned chicken breast halves
- 1/2 cup chopped roma (plum) tomatoes
- salt and pepper to taste
- 1 teaspoon balsamic vinegar, or to taste
- 1/2 pound fresh asparagus, trimmed and cut into 2 inch pieces
- 1/2 cup shredded mozzarella cheese
- 1 (7 ounce) jar roasted red peppers, drained and chopped

DIRECTIONS

1. Heat the broth in a large skillet over medium-high heat. Season chicken with salt and pepper, and place in the skillet. Cook 15 minutes, until chicken is almost done.
2. Place asparagus, red peppers and garlic in skillet. Continue cooking 10 minutes, or until chicken juices run clear and asparagus is tender. Place tomatoes in skillet during last 2 minutes of cook time. Sprinkle with vinegar. Top with mozzarella cheese to serve.

JENNY'S GRILLED CHICKEN BREASTS

Servings: 4 | Prep: 15m | Cooks: 30m | Total: 45m

NUTRITION FACTS

Calories: 139 | Carbohydrates: 3g | Fat: 1.5g | Protein: 27.4g | Cholesterol: 68mg

INGREDIENTS

- 4 skinless, boneless chicken breast halves
- ground black pepper to taste
- 1/2 cup lemon juice
- seasoning salt to taste
- 1/2 teaspoon onion powder
- 2 teaspoons dried parsley

DIRECTIONS

1. Preheat an outdoor grill for medium-high heat, and lightly oil grate.
2. Dip chicken in lemon juice, and sprinkle with the onion powder, ground black pepper, seasoning salt and parsley. Discard any remaining lemon juice.
3. Cook on the prepared grill 10 to 15 minutes per side, or until no longer pink and juices run clear.

ITALIAN PEAS

Servings: 6 | Prep: 5m | Cooks: 10m | Total: 15m

NUTRITION FACTS

Calories: 106 | Carbohydrates: 21.3g | Fat: 4.8g | Protein: 1.6g | Cholesterol: 0mg

INGREDIENTS

- 2 tablespoons olive oil
- 16 ounces frozen green peas
- 1 onion, chopped
- 1 tablespoon chicken stock
- 2 cloves garlic, minced
- salt and ground black pepper to taste

DIRECTIONS

1. Heat olive oil in a skillet over medium heat. Stir in onion; cook until softened, about 5 minutes. Stir in garlic and cook for 1 minute. Add frozen peas, and stir in stock. Season with salt and pepper. Cover, and cook until the peas are tender, about 5 minutes.

GREEN BEAN CASSEROLE

Servings: 6 | Prep: 5m | Cooks: 30m | Total: 35m

NUTRITION FACTS

Calories: 168 | Carbohydrates: 15.2g | Fat: 10.3g | Protein: 3g | Cholesterol: 2mg

INGREDIENTS

- 2 (15 ounce) cans cut green beans, drained
- 1 (2.8 ounce) can French fried onions
- 3/4 cup milk
- salt and pepper to taste
- 1 (10.75 ounce) can condensed cream of mushroom soup

DIRECTIONS

1. Preheat oven to 350 degrees F (175 degrees C).
2. In a medium casserole dish mix together green beans, milk, cream of mushroom soup, and 1/2 of the can of onions.
3. Bake for 25 minutes in the preheated oven, until heated through and bubbly. Sprinkle remaining onions over the top, and return to the oven for 5 minutes. Season with salt and pepper to taste.

SLOW COOKER CHICKEN MARRAKESH

Servings: 8 | Prep: 25m | Cooks: 4h | Total: 4h25m

NUTRITION FACTS

Calories: 290 | Carbohydrates: 36g | Fat: 2g | Protein: 30.6g | Cholesterol: 66mg

INGREDIENTS

- 1 onion, sliced
- 1/2 teaspoon ground turmeric
- 2 cloves garlic, minced (optional)
- 1/4 teaspoon ground cinnamon
- 2 large carrots, peeled and diced
- 1/2 teaspoon ground black pepper

- 2 large sweet potatoes, peeled and diced
- 1 teaspoon dried parsley
- 1 (15 ounce) can garbanzo beans, drained and rinsed
- 1 teaspoon salt
- 2 pounds skinless, boneless chicken breast halves, cut into 2-inch pieces
- 1 (14.5 ounce) can diced tomatoes
- 1/2 teaspoon ground cumin

DIRECTIONS

1. Place the onion, garlic, carrots, sweet potatoes, garbanzo beans, and chicken breast pieces into a slow cooker. In a bowl, mix the cumin, turmeric, cinnamon, black pepper, parsley, and salt, and sprinkle over the chicken and vegetables. Pour in the tomatoes, and stir to combine.
2. Cover the cooker, set to High, and cook until the sweet potatoes are tender and the sauce has thickened, 4 to 5 hours.

ORANGE GLAZED CARROTS

Servings: 4 | Prep: 5m | Cooks: 15m | Total: 20m

NUTRITION FACTS

Calories: 136 | Carbohydrates: 20.8g | Fat: 5.9g | Protein: 0.9g | Cholesterol: 15mg

INGREDIENTS

- 1 pound baby carrots
- 2 tablespoons butter
- 1/4 cup orange juice
- 1 pinch salt
- 3 tablespoons brown sugar

DIRECTIONS

1. Place carrots in a shallow saucepan, and cover with water. Boil until tender. Drain, and return carrots to pan.
2. Pour orange juice over carrots, and mix well. Simmer over medium heat for about 5 minutes. Stir in brown sugar, butter, and salt. Heat until butter and sugar melt.

PICO DE GALLO

Servings: 12 | Prep: 20m | Cooks: 3h | Total: 3h20m | Additional: 3h

NUTRITION FACTS

Calories: 10 | Carbohydrates: 2.2g | Fat: 0.1g | Protein: 0.4g | Cholesterol: 0mg

INGREDIENTS

- 6 roma (plum) tomatoes, diced
- 1 clove garlic, minced
- 1/2 red onion, minced
- 1 pinch garlic powder
- 3 tablespoons chopped fresh cilantro
- 1 pinch ground cumin, or to taste
- 1/2 jalapeno pepper, seeded and minced
- salt and ground black pepper to taste
- 1/2 lime, juiced

DIRECTIONS

1. Stir the tomatoes, onion, cilantro, jalapeno pepper, lime juice, garlic, garlic powder, cumin, salt, and pepper together in a bowl. Refrigerate at least 3 hours before serving.

YAKISOBA CHICKEN

Servings: 6 | Prep: 15m | Cooks: 15m | Total: 30m

NUTRITION FACTS

Calories: 295 | Carbohydrates: 40.7g | Fat: 4.8g | Protein: 26.3g | Cholesterol: 46mg

INGREDIENTS

- 1/2 teaspoon sesame oil
- 1/2 cup soy sauce
- 1 tablespoon canola oil
- 1 onion, sliced lengthwise into eighths
- 2 tablespoons chile paste
- 1/2 medium head cabbage, coarsely chopped
- 2 cloves garlic, chopped
- 2 carrots, coarsely chopped
- 4 skinless, boneless chicken breast halves - cut into 1 inch cubes
- 8 ounces soba noodles, cooked and drained

DIRECTIONS

1. In a large skillet combine sesame oil, canola oil and chili paste; stir-fry 30 seconds. Add garlic and stir fry an additional 30 seconds. Add chicken and 1/4 cup of the soy sauce and stir fry until chicken is no longer pink, about 5 minutes. Remove mixture from pan, set aside, and keep warm.

2. In the emptied pan combine the onion, cabbage, and carrots. Stir-fry until cabbage begins to wilt, 2 to 3 minutes. Stir in the remaining soy sauce, cooked noodles, and the chicken mixture to pan and mix to blend. Serve and enjoy!

TANGY GRILLED PORK TENDERLOIN
Servings: 6 | Prep: 15m | Cooks: 25m | Total: 4h40m | Additional: 4h

NUTRITION FACTS

Calories: 267 | Carbohydrates: 35.3g | Fat: 3.6g | Protein: 23.4g | Cholesterol: 65mg

INGREDIENTS

- 2 pounds pork tenderloin
- 1/4 teaspoon chili powder
- 2/3 cup honey
- 1/4 teaspoon salt
- 1/2 cup Dijon mustard

DIRECTIONS

1. Place meat in a large resealable plastic bag. In a medium bowl, mix together honey, Dijon mustard, chili powder, and salt. Pour marinade over tenderloins, seal, and refrigerate for at least 4 hours.

2. Prepare the grill for indirect heat.

3. Lightly oil grill grate. Remove meat from marinade, and discard liquid. Grill for 15 to 25 minutes, or until an instant-read thermometer inserted into the center reads 145 degrees F (63 degrees C).

PICO DE GALLO
Servings: 4 | Prep: 20m | Cooks: 30m | Total: 50m | Additional: 30m

NUTRITION FACTS

Calories: 21 | Carbohydrates: 4.7g | Fat: 0.1g | Protein: 0.8g | Cholesterol: 0mg

INGREDIENTS

- 1 medium tomato, diced
- 1 green onion, finely chopped
- 1 onion, finely chopped

- 1/2 teaspoon garlic powder
- 1/2 fresh jalapeno pepper, seeded and chopped
- 1/8 teaspoon salt
- 2 sprigs fresh cilantro, finely chopped
- 1/8 teaspoon pepper

DIRECTIONS

1. In a medium bowl, combine tomato, onion, jalapeno pepper (to taste,) cilantro and green onion. Season with garlic powder, salt and pepper. Stir until evenly distributed. Refrigerate for 30 minutes.

SWEET AND SPICY STIR FRY WITH CHICKEN AND BROCCOLI

Servings: 4 | Prep: 10m | Cooks: 20m | Total: 30m

NUTRITION FACTS

Calories: 156 | Carbohydrates: 10.9g | Fat: 6.2g | Protein: 15.9g | Cholesterol: 36mg

INGREDIENTS

- 3 cups broccoli florets
- 1 tablespoon low sodium soy sauce
- 1 tablespoon olive oil
- 1/2 teaspoon ground ginger
- 2 skinless, boneless chicken breast halves - cut into 1 inch strips
- 1/4 teaspoon crushed red pepper
- 1/4 cup sliced green onions
- 1/2 teaspoon salt
- 4 cloves garlic, thinly sliced
- 1/2 teaspoon black pepper
- 1 tablespoon hoisin sauce
- 1/8 cup chicken stock
- 1 tablespoon chile paste

DIRECTIONS

1. Place broccoli in a steamer over 1 inch of boiling water, and cover. Cook until tender but still firm, about 5 minutes.
2. Heat the oil in a skillet over medium heat, and saute the chicken, green onions, and garlic until the chicken is no longer pink and juices run clear.

3. Stir the hoisin sauce, chile paste, and soy sauce into the skillet; season with ginger, red pepper, salt, and black pepper. Stir in the chicken stock and simmer about 2 minutes. Mix in the steamed broccoli until coated with the sauce mixture.

APPLE PORK CHOPS

Servings: 4 | Prep: 10m | Cooks: 45m | Total: 55m

NUTRITION FACTS

Calories: 232 | Carbohydrates: 18.2g | Fat: 11.4g | Protein: 14.8g | Cholesterol: 36mg

INGREDIENTS

- 2 tablespoons vegetable oil
- 2 apples - peeled, cored and sliced
- 1/2 cup chopped onion
- 2 tablespoons brown sugar
- 4 (1/2-inch thick) pork chops
- 1/2 teaspoon ground mustard
- 1/2 teaspoon salt
- 1/8 teaspoon ground cloves
- ground black pepper to taste
- 3/4 cup hot water

DIRECTIONS

1. Preheat oven to 375 degrees F (190 degrees C).
2. Heat oil in large skillet. Saute onion in oil for 1 minute, or until tender. Remove onion and set aside. Brown pork chops on both sides in oil.
3. Place chops in an 8x12 inch baking dish and sprinkle them with salt and pepper. Cover the chops with the apples and cooked onion.
4. In a small bowl, combine brown sugar, mustard, cloves and water. Pour over chops. Cover and bake in the preheated oven for 30 to 45 minutes. Enjoy!

PERFECT SUMMER FRUIT SALAD

Servings: 10 | Prep: 25m | Cooks: 5m | Total: 3h30m

NUTRITION FACTS

Calories: 155 | Carbohydrates: 39g | Fat: 0.6g | Protein: 1.8g | Cholesterol: 0mg

INGREDIENTS

- 2/3 cup fresh orange juice
- 2 cups strawberries, hulled and sliced
- 1/3 cup fresh lemon juice
- 3 kiwi fruit, peeled and sliced
- 1/3 cup packed brown sugar
- 3 bananas, sliced
- 1/2 teaspoon grated orange zest
- 2 oranges, peeled and sectioned
- 1/2 teaspoon grated lemon zest
- 1 cup seedless grapes
- 1 teaspoon vanilla extract
- 2 cups blueberries
- 2 cups cubed fresh pineapple

DIRECTIONS

1. Bring orange juice, lemon juice, brown sugar, orange zest, and lemon zest to a boil in a saucepan over medium-high heat. Reduce heat to medium-low, and simmer until slightly thickened, about 5 minutes. Remove from heat, and stir in vanilla extract. Set aside to cool.

2. Layer the fruit in a large, clear glass bowl in this order: pineapple, strawberries, kiwi fruit, bananas, oranges, grapes, and blueberries. Pour the cooled sauce over the fruit. Cover and refrigerate for 3 to 4 hours before serving.

MANGO SALSA

Servings: 8 | Prep: 15m | Cooks: 30m | Total: 45m | Additional: 30m

NUTRITION FACTS

Calories: 21 | Carbohydrates: 5.4g | Fat: 0.1g | Protein: 0.3g | Cholesterol: 0mg

INGREDIENTS

- 1 mango - peeled, seeded, and chopped
- 1 fresh jalapeno chile pepper, finely chopped
- 1/4 cup finely chopped red bell pepper
- 2 tablespoons lime juice
- 1 green onion, chopped
- 1 tablespoon lemon juice
- 2 tablespoons chopped cilantro

DIRECTIONS

1. In a medium bowl, mix mango, red bell pepper, green onion, cilantro, jalapeno, lime juice, and lemon juice. Cover, and allow to sit at least 30 minutes before serving.

BAKED HALIBUT STEAKS

Servings: 4 | Prep: 15m | Cooks: 15m | Total: 30m

NUTRITION FACTS

Calories: 259 | Carbohydrates: 6.7g | Fat: 8g | Protein: 38.5g | Cholesterol: 66mg

INGREDIENTS

- 1 teaspoon olive oil
- 2 tablespoons chopped fresh basil
- 1 cup diced zucchini
- 1/4 teaspoon salt
- 1/2 cup minced onion
- 1/4 teaspoon ground black pepper
- 1 clove garlic, peeled and minced
- 4 (6 ounce) halibut steaks
- 2 cups diced fresh tomatoes
- 1/3 cup crumbled feta cheese

DIRECTIONS

1. Preheat oven to 450 degrees F (230 degrees C). Lightly grease a shallow baking dish.
2. Heat olive oil in a medium saucepan over medium heat and stir in zucchini, onion, and garlic. Cook and stir 5 minutes or until tender. Remove saucepan from heat and mix in tomatoes, basil, salt, and pepper.
3. Arrange halibut steaks in a single layer in the prepared baking dish. Spoon equal amounts of the zucchini mixture over each steak. Top with feta cheese.
4. Bake 15 minutes in the preheated oven, or until fish is easily flaked with a fork.

BEER LIME GRILLED CHICKEN

Servings: 4 | Prep: 10m | Cooks: 14m | Total: 54m | Additional: 30m

NUTRITION FACTS

Calories: 182 | Carbohydrates: 7g | Fat: 2.9g | Protein: 25.2g | Cholesterol: 67mg

INGREDIENTS

- 1 lime, juiced
- 2 tablespoons chopped fresh cilantro
- 1 (12 fluid ounce) can light colored beer
- Salt and pepper
- 1 teaspoon honey
- 4 skinless, boneless chicken breast halves
- 2 cloves garlic, minced

DIRECTIONS

1. In a bowl, mix the lime juice, beer, honey, garlic, cilantro, and salt and pepper until the honey dissolves. Pour the mixture over the chicken, cover and marinate for 30 minutes.
2. Preheat an outdoor grill for medium heat and lightly oil grate.
3. Remove chicken from marinade and shake off excess; discard remaining marinade. Grill chicken until tender and juices run clear, about 7 minutes per side.

GRANDMA JEANETTE'S AMAZING GERMAN RED CABBAGE

Servings: 4 | Prep: 20m | Cooks: 1h30m | Total: 1h50m

NUTRITION FACTS

Calories: 148 | Carbohydrates: 23.6g | Fat: 6g | Protein: 1.4g | Cholesterol: 15mg

INGREDIENTS

- 2 tablespoons butter
- 1/4 cup white sugar
- 5 cups shredded red cabbage
- 2 1/4 teaspoons salt
- 1 cup sliced green apples
- 1/4 teaspoon black pepper
- 1/3 cup apple cider vinegar
- 1/4 teaspoon ground cloves
- 3 tablespoons water

DIRECTIONS

1. Place butter, cabbage, apples, and sugar into a large pot. Pour in the vinegar and water, and season with salt, pepper, and clove.

2. Bring to a boil over medium-high heat, then reduce heat to low, cover, and simmer until the cabbage is tender, 1 1/2 to 2 hours.

CRUNCHY OVEN FRIED TILAPIA

Servings: 4 | Prep: 15m | Cooks: 15m | Total: 30m

NUTRITION FACTS

Calories: 209 | Carbohydrates: 18g | Fat: 2.1g | Protein: 27.5g | Cholesterol: 42mg

INGREDIENTS

- 1/4 cup all-purpose flour
- 1 pound tilapia fillets
- 1/4 teaspoon salt
- 1/4 cup dried bread crumbs
- pepper
- 1/4 cup cornmeal
- 2 egg whites
- 1/2 teaspoon dried basil, crushed

DIRECTIONS

1. Preheat oven to 450 degrees F (230 degrees Celsius).
2. Sift or stir flour, salt, and pepper together in a shallow dish, and set aside. In a bowl, beat egg whites until white and frothy. In another bowl, combine bread crumbs with cornmeal and basil.
3. To bread the fillets, dip first into flour, shaking off any excess, then into egg whites, then into bread crumb mixture.
4. Spray a shallow baking dish with non-stick cooking spray. Lay fillets flat in the dish, tucking under any thinner ends or edges for more even cooking. Bake in the preheated oven for 10 to 15 minutes, or until fish flakes easily with a folk.

BAINGAN BHARTA (EGGPLANT CURRY)

Servings: 4 | Prep: 15m | Cooks: 45m | Total: 1h

NUTRITION FACTS

Calories: 146 | Carbohydrates: 15.2g | Fat: 8g | Protein: 4g | Cholesterol: 2mg

INGREDIENTS

- 1 large eggplant
- 1 tomato, diced
- 2 tablespoons vegetable oil

- 1/2 cup plain yogurt
- 1 teaspoon cumin seeds
- 1 fresh jalapeno chile pepper, finely chopped
- 1 medium onion, thinly sliced
- 1 teaspoon salt
- 1 tablespoon ginger garlic paste
- 1/4 bunch cilantro, finely chopped
- 1 tablespoon curry powder

DIRECTIONS

1. Preheat oven to 450 degrees F (230 degrees C).
2. Place eggplant on a medium baking sheet. Bake 20 to 30 minutes in the preheated oven, until tender. Remove from heat, cool, peel, and chop.
3. Heat oil in a medium saucepan over medium heat. Mix in cumin seeds and onion. Cook and stir until onion is tender.
4. Mix ginger garlic paste, curry powder, and tomato into the saucepan, and cook about 1 minute. Stir in yogurt. Mix in eggplant and jalapeno pepper, and season with salt. Cover, and cook 10 minutes over high heat. Remove cover, reduce heat to low, and continue cooking about 5 minutes. Garnish with cilantro to serve.

T'S SWEET POTATO FRIES

Servings: 4 | Prep: 20m | Cooks: 35m | Total: 55m

NUTRITION FACTS

Calories: 174 | Carbohydrates: 26.7g | Fat: 6.9g | Protein: 2.1g | Cholesterol: 0mg

INGREDIENTS

- 4 sweet potatoes, cut into large French fries
- 1/2 teaspoon lemon pepper
- 1 tablespoon water
- 1 pinch salt and pepper to taste
- 2 teaspoons Italian seasoning
- 2 tablespoons olive oil

DIRECTIONS

1. Preheat the oven to 400 degrees F (200 degrees C).
2. Place the cut sweet potatoes into a microwave-safe dish with the water. Cook on in the microwave for 5 minutes on full power. Drain off liquid, and toss with Italian seasoning, lemon pepper, salt, pepper, and olive oil. Arrange fries on a baking sheet in a single layer.

3. Bake for 30 minutes, turning once, or until fries are crispy on the outside.

ONION RICE

Servings: 6 | Prep: 10m | Cooks: 30m | Total: 40m

NUTRITION FACTS

Calories: 141 | Carbohydrates: 26.6g | Fat: 2.5g | Protein: 2.4g | Cholesterol: 0mg

INGREDIENTS

- 1 tablespoon vegetable oil
- 1 teaspoon ground black pepper
- 1 red onion, chopped
- 2 cups chicken broth
- 1 cup long-grain white rice

DIRECTIONS

1. Heat the oil in a saucepan over medium heat. Stir in the onion, and cook until almost tender. Stir in rice, and continue cooking until coated with oil. When onion is tender and rice begins to brown lightly, season with pepper, and pour in the broth. Bring to a boil. Reduce heat to low, cover, and simmer 20 minutes.

EASY GRILLED CHICKEN TERIYAKI

Servings: 4 | Prep: 15m | Cooks: 15m | Total: 1d | Additional: 1d

NUTRITION FACTS

Calories: 240 | Carbohydrates: 16.6g | Fat: 7.5g | Protein: 25.2g | Cholesterol: 67mg

INGREDIENTS

- 4 skinless, boneless chicken breast halves
- 2 teaspoons minced fresh garlic
- 1 cup teriyaki sauce
- 2 teaspoons sesame oil
- 1/4 cup lemon juice

DIRECTIONS

1. Place chicken, teriyaki sauce, lemon juice, garlic, and sesame oil in a large resealable plastic bag. Seal bag, and shake to coat. Place in refrigerator for 24 hours, turning every so often.

2. Preheat grill for high heat.

3. Lightly oil the grill grate. Remove chicken from bag, discarding any remaining marinade. Grill for 6 to 8 minutes each side, or until juices run clear when chicken is pierced with a fork.

SLOW COOKER SWISS STEAK

Servings: 6 | Prep: 15m | Cooks: 10h15m | Total: 10h30m

NUTRITION FACTS

Calories: 246 | Carbohydrates: 19.2g | Fat: 10.6g | Protein: 16.8g | Cholesterol: 39mg

INGREDIENTS

- 1/4 cup all-purpose flour
- 1 onion, chopped
- salt and pepper to taste
- 3 carrots, shredded
- 1 1/2 pounds round steak, cut into small pieces
- 2 (14.5 ounce) cans diced tomatoes with juice
- 3 tablespoons vegetable oil
- 1 tablespoon Worcestershire sauce
- 3 stalks celery, chopped
- 2 tablespoons brown sugar, or to taste

DIRECTIONS

1. In a shallow bowl, mix the flour, salt, and pepper. Lightly coat the round steak pieces in the flour mixture.

2. Heat the oil in a skillet over medium heat, and saute the celery, onion, and carrots about 5 minutes, until tender. Remove from heat, and set aside. Mix in the round steak pieces, and cook until lightly browned.

3. Place the vegetables and steak in a slow cooker. Mix in the tomatoes with juice, Worcestershire sauce, and brown sugar.

4. Cover, and cook 8 to 10 hours on Low, until the round steak is very tender.

JAPANESE-STYLE SESAME GREEN BEANS

Servings: 4 | Prep: 5m | Cooks: 15m | Total: 20m

NUTRITION FACTS

Calories: 97 | Carbohydrates: 8.9g | Fat: 6.6g | Protein: 2.7g | Cholesterol: 0mg

INGREDIENTS

- 1 tablespoon canola oil
- 1 tablespoon soy sauce
- 1 1/2 teaspoons sesame oil
- 1 tablespoon toasted sesame seeds
- 1 pound fresh green beans, washed

DIRECTIONS

1. Warm a large skillet or wok over medium heat. When the skillet is hot, pour in canola and sesame oils, then place whole green beans into the skillet. Stir the beans to coat with oil. Cook until the beans are bright green and slightly browned in spots, about 10 minutes. Remove from heat, and stir in soy sauce; cover, and let sit about 5 minutes. Transfer to a serving platter, and sprinkle with toasted sesame seeds.

BAKED TOFU BITES

Servings: 4 | Prep: 10m | Cooks: 15m | Total: 25m

NUTRITION FACTS

Calories: 168 | Carbohydrates: 12.8g | Fat: 8.8g | Protein: 12.7g | Cholesterol: 0mg

INGREDIENTS

- 1 (16 ounce) package extra firm tofu
- 1 dash hot sauce
- 1/4 cup soy sauce
- 1 tablespoon sesame seeds
- 2 tablespoons maple syrup
- 1/4 teaspoon garlic powder
- 2 tablespoons ketchup
- 1/4 teaspoon ground black pepper
- 1 tablespoon vinegar
- 1 teaspoon liquid smoke flavoring

DIRECTIONS

1. Preheat oven to 375 degrees F (190 degrees C). Lightly spray a non-stick baking sheet with oil.
2. Slice tofu into 1/2-inch slices, and gently press excess water out of tofu. Cut sliced tofu into 1/2-inch cubes.

3. In a bowl, stir together the soy sauce, maple syrup, ketchup, vinegar, and hot sauce. Stir in sesame seeds, garlic powder, black pepper, and liquid smoke. Gently stir tofu cubes into sauce. Cover, and marinate at least 5 minutes.

4. Place the tofu on the baking sheet in a single layer. Bake in a preheated oven for 15 minutes. Turn tofu, and bake until the tofu turns golden brown, about 15 minutes more.

BALSAMIC GLAZED CARROTS

Servings: 4 | Prep: 5m | Cooks: 10m | Total: 15m

NUTRITION FACTS

Calories: 82 | Carbohydrates: 12.5g | Fat: 3.5g | Protein: 0.7g | Cholesterol: 0mg

INGREDIENTS

- 3 cups baby carrots
- 1 1/2 tablespoons balsamic vinegar
- 1 tablespoon olive oil
- 1 tablespoon brown sugar

DIRECTIONS

1. Heat oil in a skillet over medium-high heat. Saute carrots in oil for about 10 minutes, or until tender. Stir in balsamic vinegar and brown sugar, mix to coat and serve.

ROASTED ASPARAGUS WITH PARMESAN

Servings: 4 | Prep: 5m | Cooks: 15m | Total: 20m

NUTRITION FACTS

Calories: 46 | Carbohydrates: 4.7g | Fat: 1.7g | Protein: 4.4g | Cholesterol: 4mg

INGREDIENTS

- olive oil cooking spray
- 1 teaspoon sea salt
- 1 pound fresh asparagus, tough ends trimmed
- 1/4 teaspoon garlic powder, or to taste
- 1/4 cup shredded Parmesan cheese

DIRECTIONS

1. Preheat oven to 400 degrees F (200 degrees C).

2. Spray the inside of a 9x13 casserole dish with olive oil cooking spray. Place asparagus in the dish and lightly spray spears with cooking spray.

3. Sprinkle asparagus with Parmesan cheese, sea salt, and garlic powder.

4. Roast in preheated oven until fork easily punctures thickest part of stem, about 12 minutes.

SLOW COOKER HONEY GARLIC CHICKEN
Servings: 10 | Prep: 20m | Cooks: 4h | Total: 4h20m

NUTRITION FACTS

Calories: 235 | Carbohydrates: 34.4g | Fat: 6g | Protein: 13g | Cholesterol: 42mg

INGREDIENTS

- 1 tablespoon vegetable oil
- 2 cloves garlic, crushed
- 10 boneless, skinless chicken thighs
- 1 tablespoon minced fresh ginger root
- 3/4 cup honey
- 1 (20 ounce) can pineapple tidbits, drained with juice reserved
- 3/4 cup lite soy sauce
- 2 tablespoons cornstarch
- 3 tablespoons ketchup
- 1/4 cup water

DIRECTIONS

1. Heat oil in a skillet over medium heat, and cook chicken thighs just until evenly browned on all sides. Place thighs in a slow cooker.

2. In a bowl, mix honey, soy sauce, ketchup, garlic, ginger, and reserved pineapple juice. Pour into the slow cooker.

3. Cover, and cook 4 hours on High. Stir in pineapple tidbits just before serving.

4. Mix the cornstarch and water in a small bowl. Remove thighs from slow cooker. Blend the cornstarch mixture into remaining sauce in the slow cooker to thicken. Serve sauce over the chicken.

BAKED WHOLE CAULIFLOWER
Servings: 6 | Prep: 5m | Cooks: 40m | Total: 45m

NUTRITION FACTS

Calories: 149 | Carbohydrates: 14.7g | Fat: 8.7g | Protein: 5g | Cholesterol: 2mg

INGREDIENTS

- 1 large head cauliflower
- 1/8 teaspoon garlic powder
- 1/2 cup seasoned bread crumbs
- 1/8 teaspoon salt
- 2 tablespoons grated Parmesan cheese
- 1 pinch red pepper flakes
- 1/4 cup margarine, melted
- 1 pinch dried oregano

DIRECTIONS

1. Clean cauliflower, and trim off leaves and any brown spots. Place the whole head of cauliflower into a steamer basket, place the basket in a large pot, and add one inch of water. Cover, and bring to a boil over medium heat. Cook for about 20 minutes or until tender.
2. Preheat the oven to 375 degrees F (190 degrees C). In a medium bowl, mix together the bread crumbs, Parmesan cheese, melted margarine. Season with garlic powder, salt, red pepper flakes, and oregano, and mix well. Place the head of cauliflower into a baking dish, and coat with the breadcrumb mixture.
3. Bake for about 10 to 15 minutes in the preheated oven, or until golden brown.

STOVETOP MOROCCAN TAGINE

Servings: 6 | Prep: 15m | Cooks: 45m | Total: 1h

NUTRITION FACTS

Calories: 265 | Carbohydrates: 44.7g | Fat: 4.3g | Protein: 14.1g | Cholesterol: 20mg

INGREDIENTS

- 1 tablespoon olive oil
- 1 (14.5 ounce) can diced tomatoes with juice
- 2 skinless, boneless chicken breast halves - cut into chunks
- 1 (14 ounce) can vegetable broth
- 1/2 onion, chopped
- 1 tablespoon sugar
- 3 cloves garlic, minced
- 1 tablespoon lemon juice
- 1 small butternut squash, peeled and chopped
- 1 teaspoon salt
- 1 (15.5 ounce) can garbanzo beans, drained and rinsed
- 1 teaspoon ground coriander

- 1 carrot, peeled and chopped
- 1 dash cayenne pepper

DIRECTIONS

1. Heat the olive oil in a large skillet over medium heat, and cook the chicken, onion, and garlic about 15 minutes, until browned.
2. Mix the squash, garbanzo beans, carrot, tomatoes with juice, broth, sugar, and lemon juice into the skillet. Season with salt, coriander, and cayenne pepper. Bring the mixture to a boil, and continue cooking 30 minutes, until vegetables are tender.

LENTILS AND SPINACH

Servings: 4 | Prep: 10m | Cooks: 55m | Total: 1h5m

NUTRITION FACTS

Calories: 165 | Carbohydrates: 24g | Fat: 4.3g | Protein: 9.7g | Cholesterol: 0mg

INGREDIENTS

- 1 tablespoon vegetable oil
- 1 (10 ounce) package frozen spinach
- 2 white onions, halved and sliced into 1/2 rings
- 1 teaspoon salt
- 3 cloves garlic, minced
- 1 teaspoon ground cumin
- 1/2 cup lentils
- freshly ground black pepper to taste
- 2 cups water
- 2 cloves garlic, crushed

DIRECTIONS

1. Heat oil in a heavy pan over medium heat. Saute onion for 10 minutes or so, until it begins to turn golden. Add minced garlic and saute for another minute or so.
2. Add lentils and water to the saucepan. Bring mixture to a boil. Cover, lower heat, and simmer about 35 minutes, until lentils are soft (this may take less time, depending on your water and the lentils).
3. Meanwhile cook the spinach in microwave according to package directions. Add spinach, salt and cumin to the saucepan. Cover and simmer until all is heated, about ten minutes. Grind in plenty of pepper and press in extra garlic to taste.

ARTICHOKE AND SUN-DRIED TOMATO CHICKEN

Servings: 4 | Prep: 10m | Cooks: 25m | Total: 35m

NUTRITION FACTS

Calories: 228 | Carbohydrates: 11.4g | Fat: 6.5g | Protein: 30.5g | Cholesterol: 68mg

INGREDIENTS

- 4 skinless, boneless chicken breast halves
- 1 (14.5 ounce) can diced tomatoes with green peppers and onions
- salt and pepper to taste
- 1/4 cup sun-dried tomato pesto
- 2 teaspoons olive oil
- 1 (14 ounce) can artichoke hearts in water, drained and quartered

DIRECTIONS

1. Season both sides of chicken breasts with salt and pepper. Heat oil in a large skillet over medium-high heat. Place chicken in skillet; cook, turning once to brown each side. Remove chicken from pan, and set aside.
2. Pour tomatoes into pan; cook for 1 minute, stirring constantly, and incorporating any brown bits from bottom of pan. Stir in pesto and artichokes, and return chicken to pan. Cover, and reduce heat to medium. Simmer for 5 to 10 minutes, or until chicken is cooked through.

TASTY COLLARD GREENS

Servings: 10 | Prep: 30m | Cooks: 2h | Total: 2h30m

NUTRITION FACTS

Calories: 142 | Carbohydrates: 10.6g | Fat: 7.9g | Protein: 9.6g | Cholesterol: 23mg

INGREDIENTS

- 1/4 cup olive oil
- 5 bunches collard greens - rinsed, trimmed and chopped
- 2 tablespoons minced garlic
- salt and black pepper to taste
- 5 cups chicken stock
- 1 tablespoon crushed red pepper flakes (optional)
- 1 smoked turkey drumstick

DIRECTIONS

1. Heat olive oil in a large pot over medium heat. Add garlic, and gently saute until light brown. Pour in the chicken stock, and add the turkey leg. Cover the pot, and simmer for 30 minutes.

2. Add the collard greens to the cooking pot, and turn the heat up to medium-high. Let the greens cook down for about 45 minutes, stirring occasionally.

3. Reduce heat to medium, and season with salt and pepper to taste. Continue to cook until the greens are tender and dark green, 45 to 60 minutes. Drain greens, reserving liquid. Mix in red pepper flakes if desired. Use liquid to reheat leftovers.

ESPINACAS CON GARBANZOS (SPINACH WITH GARBANZO BEANS)

Servings: 4 | Prep: 15m | Cooks: 10m | Total: 25m

NUTRITION FACTS

Calories: 169 | Carbohydrates: 26g | Fat: 4.9g | Protein: 7.3g | Cholesterol: 0mg

INGREDIENTS

- 1 tablespoon extra-virgin olive oil
- 1 (12 ounce) can garbanzo beans, drained
- 4 cloves garlic, minced
- 1/2 teaspoon cumin
- 1/2 onion, diced
- 1/2 teaspoon salt
- 1 (10 ounce) box frozen chopped spinach, thawed and drained well

DIRECTIONS

1. Heat the olive oil in a skillet over medium-low heat. Cook the garlic and onion in the oil until translucent, about 5 minutes. Stir in the spinach, garbanzo beans, cumin, and salt. Use your stirring spoon to lightly mash the beans as the mixture cooks. Allow to cook until thoroughly heated.

GRILLED PEANUT CHICKEN

Servings: 4 | Prep: 15m | Cooks: 15m | Total: 30m

NUTRITION FACTS

Calories: 176 | Carbohydrates: 3.6g | Fat: 5.6g | Protein: 27g | Cholesterol: 67mg

INGREDIENTS

- 2 tablespoons reduced fat peanut butter

- 1/3 teaspoon curry powder
- 1 tablespoon fresh lime juice
- 1 dash ground cayenne pepper
- 2 teaspoons soy sauce
- 4 skinless, boneless chicken breast halves
- 1 clove garlic, chopped

DIRECTIONS

1. Preheat grill for high heat.
2. In a bowl, mix the peanut butter, lime juice, soy sauce, garlic, curry powder, and cayenne pepper.
3. Lightly oil the grill grate. Place chicken on grate, and brush with 1/2 the sauce. Grill 6 to 8 minutes. Turn chicken, and brush with remaining sauce. Continue grilling 6 to 8 minutes, until chicken juices run clear.

ASIAN TUNA PATTIES

Servings: 6 | Prep: 15m | Cooks: 20m | Total: 35m

NUTRITION FACTS

Calories: 214 | Carbohydrates: 21.1g | Fat: 7.5g | Protein: 15g | Cholesterol: 44mg

INGREDIENTS

- 2 (5 ounce) cans tuna, drained and flaked
- 1 tablespoon teriyaki sauce
- 1 egg, beaten
- 1 tablespoon ketchup
- 3/4 cup dry bread crumbs
- 1 teaspoon sesame oil
- 3 green onions, minced
- 1 teaspoon black pepper
- 1 clove garlic, peeled and minced
- 1/2 cup cornmeal
- 1 tablespoon soy sauce
- 2 tablespoons vegetable oil

DIRECTIONS

1. In a large bowl, mix tuna, egg, bread crumbs, green onions, and garlic. Blend soy sauce, teriyaki sauce, ketchup, sesame oil, and pepper into the mixture. Form the mixture into about 6 patties approximately 1 inch thick. Lightly sprinkle each patty on all sides with cornmeal.

2. Heat oil in a medium skillet over medium heat. Fry each patty about 5 minutes on each side, until golden brown.

TASTY COLLARD GREENS
Servings: 10 | Prep: 30m | Cooks: 2h | Total: 2h30m

NUTRITION FACTS

Calories: 142 | Carbohydrates: 10.6g | Fat: 7.9g | Protein: 9.6g | Cholesterol: 23mg

INGREDIENTS

- 1/4 cup olive oil
- 5 bunches collard greens - rinsed, trimmed and chopped
- 2 tablespoons minced garlic
- salt and black pepper to taste
- 5 cups chicken stock
- 1 tablespoon crushed red pepper flakes (optional)
- 1 smoked turkey drumstick

DIRECTIONS

1. Heat olive oil in a large pot over medium heat. Add garlic, and gently saute until light brown. Pour in the chicken stock, and add the turkey leg. Cover the pot, and simmer for 30 minutes.
2. Add the collard greens to the cooking pot, and turn the heat up to medium-high. Let the greens cook down for about 45 minutes, stirring occasionally.
3. Reduce heat to medium, and season with salt and pepper to taste. Continue to cook until the greens are tender and dark green, 45 to 60 minutes. Drain greens, reserving liquid. Mix in red pepper flakes if desired. Use liquid to reheat leftovers.

COLA CHOPS
Servings: 8 | Prep: 15m | Cooks: 1h | Total: 1h15m

NUTRITION FACTS

Calories: 190 | Carbohydrates: 17.6g | Fat: 3.9g | Protein: 20.9g | Cholesterol: 65mg

INGREDIENTS

- 8 pork chops
- 1 cup ketchup
- 1 cup cola-flavored carbonated beverage

- 4 tablespoons brown sugar

DIRECTIONS

1. Preheat oven to 350 degrees F (175 degrees C).
2. Place pork chops in a 9x13 inch baking dish. In a small bowl, mix together the cola and ketchup. Pour over chops and sprinkle with brown sugar. Bake uncovered for about 1 hour, or until pork is cooked through and internal temperature has reached 145 degrees F (63 degrees C).

VEGAN BEAN TACO FILLING
Servings: 8 | Prep: 15m | Cooks: 15m | Total: 30m

NUTRITION FACTS

Calories: 142 | Carbohydrates: 24g | Fat: 2.5g | Protein: 7.5g | Cholesterol: 0mg

INGREDIENTS

- 1 tablespoon olive oil
- 1 1/2 tablespoons cumin
- 1 onion, diced
- 1 teaspoon paprika
- 2 cloves garlic, minced
- 1 teaspoon cayenne pepper
- 1 bell pepper, chopped
- 1 teaspoon chili powder
- 2 (14.5 ounce) cans black beans, rinsed, drained, and mashed
- 1 cup salsa
- 2 tablespoons yellow cornmeal

DIRECTIONS

1. Heat olive oil in a medium skillet over medium heat. Stir in onion, garlic, and bell pepper; cook until tender. Stir in mashed beans. Add the cornmeal. Mix in cumin, paprika, cayenne, chili powder, and salsa. Cover, and cook 5 minutes.

DAD'S PAN-FRIED GREEN BEANS
Servings: 6 | Prep: 10m | Cooks: 10m | Total: 20m

NUTRITION FACTS

Calories: 73 | Carbohydrates: 7.5g | Fat: 4.6g | Protein: 1.9g | Cholesterol: 0mg

INGREDIENTS

- 1 pound fresh green beans, trimmed
- 1 teaspoon white sugar
- 3 tablespoons light soy sauce
- 2 tablespoons sesame oil
- 1 tablespoon balsamic vinegar
- 2 teaspoons minced garlic

DIRECTIONS

1. Place the green beans in a large saucepan or pot with one inch of water. You may place them in a steamer insert if you have one. Bring to a boil, cover and cook for 5 minutes, they should still be firm and bright green.
2. In a small bowl, stir together the soy sauce, balsamic vinegar and sugar; set aside.
3. Heat the sesame oil in a large skillet over medium heat. Add garlic and cook until starting to brown. Add the green beans and stir to coat with the oil. Stir in the soy sauce mixture and simmer for a couple of minutes uncovered to reduce the sauce. Transfer the beans to a serving dish and pour the sauce over them.

FISH IN FOIL

Servings: 2 | Prep: 10m | Cooks: 10m | Total: 30m

NUTRITION FACTS

Calories: 213 | Carbohydrates: 7.5g | Fat: 10.9g | Protein: 24.3g | Cholesterol: 67mg

INGREDIENTS

- 2 rainbow trout fillets
- 1 teaspoon ground black pepper
- 1 tablespoon olive oil
- 1 fresh jalapeno pepper, sliced
- 2 teaspoons garlic salt
- 1 lemon, sliced

DIRECTIONS

1. Preheat oven to 400 degrees F (200 degrees C). Rinse fish, and pat dry.
2. Rub fillets with olive oil, and season with garlic salt and black pepper. Place each fillet on a large sheet of aluminum foil. Top with jalapeno slices, and squeeze the juice from the ends of the lemons over the fish. Arrange lemon slices on top of fillets. Carefully seal all edges of the foil to form enclosed packets. Place packets on baking sheet.

3. Bake in preheated oven for 15 to 20 minutes, depending on the size of fish. Fish is done when it flakes easily with a fork.

SPICED SLOW COOKER APPLESAUCE

Servings: 8 | Prep: 10m | Cooks: 6h30m | Total: 6h40m

NUTRITION FACTS

Calories: 150 | Carbohydrates: 39.4g | Fat: 0.2g | Protein: 0.4g | Cholesterol: 0mg

INGREDIENTS

- 8 apples - peeled, cored, and thinly sliced
- 3/4 cup packed brown sugar
- 1/2 cup water
- 1/2 teaspoon pumpkin pie spice

DIRECTIONS

3. Combine the apples and water in a slow cooker; cook on Low for 6 to 8 hours. Stir in the brown sugar and pumpkin pie spice; continue cooking another 30 minutes.

WONTON SOUP

Servings: 8 | Prep: 30m | Cooks: 5m | Total: 1h15m | Additional 40m

NUTRITION FACTS

Calories: 145 | Carbohydrates: 15.3g | Fat: 4.2g | Protein: 9.9g | Cholesterol: 33mg

INGREDIENTS

- 1/2 pound boneless pork loin, coarsely chopped
- 1 teaspoon finely chopped green onion
- 2 ounces peeled shrimp, finely chopped
- 1 teaspoon chopped fresh ginger root
- 1 teaspoon brown sugar
- 24 (3.5 inch square) wonton wrappers
- 1 tablespoon Chinese rice wine
- 3 cups chicken stock
- 1 tablespoon light soy sauce
- 1/8 cup finely chopped green onion

DIRECTIONS

1. In a large bowl, combine pork, shrimp, sugar, wine, soy sauce, 1 teaspoon chopped green onion and ginger. Blend well, and let stand for 25 to 30 minutes.
2. Place about one teaspoon of the filling at the center of each wonton skin. Moisten all 4 edges of wonton wrapper with water, then pull the top corner down to the bottom, folding the wrapper over the filling to make a triangle. Press edges firmly to make a seal. Bring left and right corners together above the filling. Overlap the tips of these corners, moisten with water and press together. Continue until all wrappers are used.
3. FOR SOUP: Bring the chicken stock to a rolling boil. Drop wontons in, and cook for 5 minutes. Garnish with chopped green onion, and serve.

HONEY ORANGE GREEN BEANS
Servings: 6 | Prep: 15m | Cooks: 10m | Total: 25m

NUTRITION FACTS

Calories: 91 | Carbohydrates: 14.5g | Fat: 3.2g | Protein: 4.6g | Cholesterol: 0mg

INGREDIENTS

- 12 cups chopped kale
- 1 teaspoon soy sauce
- 2 tablespoons lemon juice
- salt to taste
- 1 tablespoon olive oil, or as needed
- ground black pepper to taste
- 1 tablespoon minced garlic

DIRECTIONS

1. Place a steamer insert into a saucepan, and fill with water to just below the bottom of the steamer. Cover, and bring the water to a boil over high heat. Add the kale, recover, and steam until just tender, 7 to 10 minutes depending on thickness.
2. Whisk together the lemon juice, olive oil, garlic, soy sauce, salt, and black pepper in a large bowl. Toss steamed kale into dressing until well coated.

A JERKY CHICKEN
Servings: 4 | Prep: 1h | Cooks: 15m | Total: 1h15m

NUTRITION FACTS

Calories: 197 | Carbohydrates: 13.5g | Fat: 2.7g | Protein: 28.5g | Cholesterol: 68mg

INGREDIENTS

- 1 teaspoon onion, finely chopped
- 1 teaspoon sesame oil
- 3 tablespoons brown sugar
- 3 cloves garlic, chopped
- 4 tablespoons soy sauce
- 1/2 teaspoon ground allspice
- 4 tablespoons red wine vinegar
- 1 habanero pepper, sliced
- 2 teaspoons chopped fresh thyme
- 4 skinless, boneless chicken breast halves - cut into 1 inch strips

DIRECTIONS

1. Combine the onion, brown sugar, soy sauce, vinegar, thyme, sesame oil, garlic, allspice and habanero pepper in the container of a food processor or blender. Process until smooth. Place the chicken into a large resealable bag, and pour in 3/4 of the sauce. Squeeze out excess air, and seal. Marinate in the refrigerator for at least one hour.
2. Preheat your oven's broiler.
3. Remove chicken from bag, and discard marinade. Broil chicken for 10 to 15 minutes, turning once to ensure even cooking. Heat remaining sauce in a small pan, and pour over chicken when serving.

PASTA WITH SCALLOPS, ZUCCHINI, AND TOMATOES
Servings: 8 | Prep: 15m | Cooks: 15m | Total: 30m

NUTRITION FACTS

Calories: 335 | Carbohydrates: 46.1g | Fat: 9.1g | Protein: 18.7g | Cholesterol: 20mg

INGREDIENTS

- 1 pound dry fettuccine pasta
- 1/2 teaspoon crushed red pepper flakes
- 1/4 cup olive oil
- 1 cup chopped fresh basil
- 3 cloves garlic, minced
- 4 roma (plum) tomatoes, chopped
- 2 zucchinis, diced
- 1 pound bay scallops
- 1/2 teaspoon salt
- 2 tablespoons grated Parmesan cheese

DIRECTIONS

1. In a large pot with boiling salted water cook pasta until al dente. Drain.
2. Meanwhile, in a large skillet heat oil, add garlic and cook until tender. Add the zucchini, salt, red pepper flakes, dried basil (if using) and saute for 10 minutes. Add chopped tomatoes, bay scallops, and fresh basil (if using) and simmer for 5 minutes, or until scallops are opaque.
3. Pour sauce over cooked pasta and serve with grated Parmesan cheese.

SLOW COOKER GREEN BEANS, HAM AND POTATOES

Servings: 10 | Prep: 30m | Cooks: 4h | Total: 4h30m

NUTRITION FACTS

Calories: 200 | Carbohydrates: 20.6g | Fat: 9g | Protein: 10.2g | Cholesterol: 29mg

INGREDIENTS

- 2 pounds fresh green beans, rinsed and trimmed
- 1 teaspoon onion powder
- 1 large onion, chopped
- 1 teaspoon seasoning salt
- 3 ham hocks
- 1 tablespoon chicken bouillon granules
- 1 1/2 pounds new potatoes, quartered
- ground black pepper to taste
- 1 teaspoon garlic powder

DIRECTIONS

1. Halve beans if they are large, place in a slow cooker with water to barely cover, and add onion and ham hocks. Cover, and cook on High until simmering. Reduce heat to Low, and cook for 2 to 3 hours, or until beans are crisp but not done.
2. Add potatoes, and cook for another 45 minutes. While potatoes are cooking, remove ham hocks from slow cooker, and remove meat from bones. Chop or shred meat, and return to slow cooker. Season with garlic powder, onion powder, seasoning salt, bouillon, and pepper. Cook until potatoes are done, then adjust seasoning to taste.
3. To serve, use a slotted spoon to put beans, potatoes, and ham into a serving dish with a little broth.

SLOW COOKER OATS

Servings: 6 | Prep: 15m | Cooks: 6h | Total: 6h15m

NUTRITION FACTS

Calories: 208 | Carbohydrates: 37.2g | Fat: 5.6g | Protein: 3.9g | Cholesterol: 10mg

INGREDIENTS

- 1 cup steel cut oats
- 2 tablespoons butter
- 3 1/2 cups water
- 1 tablespoon ground cinnamon
- 1 cup peeled and chopped apple
- 2 tablespoons brown sugar
- 1/2 cup raisins
- 1 teaspoon vanilla extract

DIRECTIONS

1. Place the steel cut oats, water, apple, raisins, butter, cinnamon, brown sugar, and vanilla extract into a slow cooker, and stir to combine and dissolve the sugar. Cover the cooker, set to Low, and allow to cook 6 to 7 hours (for firm oats) or 8 hours (for softer texture).

ROASTED ASPARAGUS AND MUSHROOMS

Servings: 6 | Prep: 10m | Cooks: 15m | Total: 25m

NUTRITION FACTS

Calories: 38 | Carbohydrates: 4.3g | Fat: 1.8g | Protein: 2.8g | Cholesterol: 0mg

INGREDIENTS

- 1 bunch fresh asparagus, trimmed
- 2 teaspoons olive oil
- ½ pound fresh mushrooms, quartered
- kosher salt to taste
- 2 sprigs fresh rosemary, minced
- freshly ground black pepper to taste

DIRECTIONS

1. Preheat oven to 450 degrees F (230 degrees C). Lightly spray a cookie sheet with vegetable cooking spray.
2. Place the asparagus and mushrooms in a bowl. Drizzle with the olive oil, then season with rosemary, salt, and pepper; toss well. Lay the asparagus and mushrooms out on the prepared pan in an even layer. Roast in the preheated oven until the asparagus is tender, about 15 minutes.

TEN MINUTE SZECHUAN CHICKEN

Servings: 4 | Prep: 20m | Cooks: 10m | Total: 30m

NUTRITION FACTS

Calories: 206 | Carbohydrates: 10.1g | Fat: 4.9g | Protein: 28.7g | Cholesterol: 68mg

INGREDIENTS

- 4 boneless skinless chicken breasts, cut into cubes
- 1 1/2 tablespoons white wine vinegar
- 3 tablespoons cornstarch
- 1/4 cup water
- 1 tablespoon vegetable oil
- 1 teaspoon white sugar
- 4 cloves garlic, minced
- 3 green onions, sliced diagonally into 1/2 inch pieces
- 5 tablespoons low-sodium soy sauce
- 1/8 teaspoon cayenne pepper, or to taste

DIRECTIONS

1. Place the chicken and cornstarch into a bag or bowl, and toss to coat. Heat oil in a wok or large skillet over medium-high heat. Fry the chicken pieces and garlic, stirring constantly until lightly browned. Stir in the soy sauce, vinegar, sugar and water. Cover, and cook until the chicken pieces are no longer pink inside, 3 to 5 minutes.
2. Stir in the green onion, and cayenne pepper, cook uncovered for about 2 more minutes. Serve over white rice.

PAT'S MUSHROOM SAUTE

Servings: 4 | Prep: 5m | Cooks: 30m | Total: 35m

NUTRITION FACTS

Calories: 94 | Carbohydrates: 5.3g | Fat: 7.9g | Protein: 2.3g | Cholesterol: 15mg

INGREDIENTS

- 2 tablespoons butter
- 1 clove garlic, minced
- 1/2 tablespoon olive oil
- 1/8 teaspoon dried oregano
- 1/2 tablespoon balsamic vinegar

- 1 pound button mushrooms, sliced

DIRECTIONS

1. Melt butter with oil in a large skillet over medium heat. Stir in balsamic vinegar, garlic, oregano, and mushrooms. Saute for 20 to 30 minutes, or until tender.

GRILLED PORK TENDERLOIN

Servings: 6 | Prep: 10m | Cooks: 45m | Total: 55m

NUTRITION FACTS

Calories: 197 | Carbohydrates: 15.7g | Fat: 3.7g | Protein: 23.5g | Cholesterol: 65mg

INGREDIENTS

- 2 (1 pound) pork tenderloins
- 1 teaspoon ground black pepper
- 1 teaspoon garlic powder
- 1 cup barbeque sauce
- 1 teaspoon salt

DIRECTIONS

1. Prepare grill for indirect heat.
2. Season meat with garlic powder, salt, and pepper.
3. Lightly oil grate. Place tenderloin on grate, and position drip pan under meat. Cook over indirect heat for 30 minutes.
4. Brush tenderloin with barbeque sauce. Continue cooking for 15 minutes, or until an instant-read thermometer inserted into the center reads 145 degrees F (63 degrees C). Allow pork to rest for 10 minutes. Slice pork, and serve with additional barbeque sauce for dipping.

BAKED FRENCH FRIES

Servings: 4 | Prep: 20m | Cooks: 25m | Total: 45m

NUTRITION FACTS

Calories: 145 | Carbohydrates: 28.2g | Fat: 1.6g | Protein: 5.2g | Cholesterol: 4mg

INGREDIENTS

- 3 russet potatoes, sliced into 1/4 inch strips
- 1/4 cup grated Parmesan cheese

- cooking spray
- salt and pepper to taste
- 1 teaspoon dried basil

DIRECTIONS

1. Preheat oven to 400 degrees F (200 degrees C). Lightly grease a medium baking sheet.
2. Arrange potato strips in a single layer on the prepared baking sheet, skin sides down. Spray lightly with cooking spray, and sprinkle with basil, Parmesan cheese, salt and pepper.
3. Bake 25 minutes in the preheated oven, or until golden brown.

CAJUN PASTA FRESCA

Servings: 8 | Prep: 5m | Cooks: 20m | Total: 25m

NUTRITION FACTS

Calories: 294 | Carbohydrates: 46.2g | Fat: 7.5g | Protein: 12.2g | Cholesterol: 0mg

INGREDIENTS

- 1 pound vermicelli pasta
- 1 tablespoon chopped fresh parsley
- 2 tablespoons olive oil
- 1 tablespoon Cajun seasoning
- 1 teaspoon minced garlic
- 1/2 cup shredded mozzarella cheese
- 13 roma (plum) tomatoes, chopped
- 1/2 cup grated Parmesan cheese
- 1 tablespoon salt

DIRECTIONS

1. Bring a large pot of lightly salted water to a boil. Add pasta and cook for 8 to 10 minutes or until al dente; drain.
2. While the pasta water is boiling, in a large skillet over medium heat, briefly saute garlic in oil. Stir in tomatoes and their juice and sprinkle with salt. When tomatoes are bubbly, mash slightly with a fork. Stir in parsley, reduce heat and simmer 5 minutes more.
3. Toss hot pasta with tomato sauce, Cajun seasoning, mozzarella and Parmesan.

SUPERFAST ASPARAGUS

Servings: 3 | Prep: 5m | Cooks: 10m | Total: 15m

NUTRITION FACTS

Calories: 32 | Carbohydrates: 6.3g | Fat: 0.2g | Protein: 3.4g | Cholesterol: 0mg

INGREDIENTS

- 1 pound asparagus
- 1 teaspoon Cajun seasoning

DIRECTIONS

1. Preheat oven to 425 degrees F (220 degrees C).
2. Snap the asparagus at the tender part of the stalk. Arrange spears in one layer on a baking sheet. Spray lightly with nonstick spray; sprinkle with the Cajun seasoning.
3. Bake in the preheated oven until tender, about 10 minutes.

RAMJAM CHICKEN

Servings: 8 | Prep: 20m | Cooks: 15m | Total: 3h35m | Additional: 3h

NUTRITION FACTS

Calories: 303 | Carbohydrates: 1.5g | Fat: 9.1g | Protein: 49.6g | Cholesterol: 134mg

INGREDIENTS

- 1/4 cup soy sauce
- 1 teaspoon grated fresh ginger root
- 3 tablespoons dry white wine
- 1 clove garlic, crushed
- 2 tablespoons lemon juice
- 1/4 teaspoon onion powder
- 2 tablespoons vegetable oil
- 1 pinch ground black pepper
- 3/4 teaspoon dried Italian-style seasoning
- 8 skinless, boneless chicken breast halves - cut into strips

DIRECTIONS

1. In a large, resealable plastic bag, combine the soy sauce, wine, lemon juice, oil, Italian-style seasoning, ginger, garlic, onion powder, and ground black pepper. Place chicken in the bag. Seal, and let marinate in the refrigerator for at least 3 hours, or overnight.
2. Preheat an outdoor grill for medium-high heat.

3. Thread the chicken onto skewers, and set aside. Pour marinade into a small saucepan, and bring to a boil over high heat.
4. Lightly oil the grill grate. Cook chicken on the prepared grill for approximately 8 minutes per side, basting with the sauce several times. Chicken is done when juices run clear.

RANCH CRISPY CHICKEN

Servings: 8 | Prep: 15m | Cooks: 30m | Total: 45m

NUTRITION FACTS

Calories: 162 | Carbohydrates: 6.1g | Fat: 1.7g | Protein: 27.8g | Cholesterol: 68mg

INGREDIENTS

- 8 skinless, boneless chicken breast halves
- 1/4 cup dry bread crumbs
- 2 (1 ounce) packages ranch dressing mix

DIRECTIONS

1. Preheat oven to 375 degrees F (190 degrees C).
2. Combine dressing mix and bread crumbs in a plastic bag. Add chicken and shake until coated.
3. Place coated chicken pieces on an ungreased cookie sheet and bake in preheated oven for 25 to 30 minutes, or until chicken is cooked through and juices run clear. Serve with rice or potatoes, if desired.

OVEN ROASTED RED POTATOES AND ASPARAGUS

Servings: 6 | Prep: 15m | Cooks: 45m | Total: 1h

NUTRITION FACTS

Calories: 149 | Carbohydrates: 23.5g | Fat: 4.9g | Protein: 4.2g | Cholesterol: 0mg

INGREDIENTS

- 1 ½ pounds red potatoes, cut into chunks
- 4 teaspoons dried thyme
- 2 tablespoons extra virgin olive oil
- 2 teaspoons kosher salt
- 8 cloves garlic, thinly sliced
- 1 bunch fresh asparagus, trimmed and cut into 1 inch pieces
- 4 teaspoons dried rosemary

- ground black pepper to taste

DIRECTIONS

1. Preheat oven to 425 degrees F (220 degrees C).
2. In a large baking dish, toss the red potatoes with 1/2 the olive oil, garlic, rosemary, thyme, and 1/2 the kosher salt. Cover with aluminum foil.
3. Bake 20 minutes in the preheated oven. Mix in the asparagus, remaining olive oil, and remaining salt. Cover, and continue cooking 15 minutes, or until the potatoes are tender. Increase oven temperature to 450 degrees F (230 degrees C). Remove foil, and continue cooking 5 to 10 minutes, until potatoes are lightly browned. Season with pepper to serve.

ROSEMARY TURKEY MEATLOAF

Servings: 8 | Prep: 15m | Cooks: 1h | Total: 1h15m

NUTRITION FACTS

Calories: 362 | Carbohydrates: 47.1g | Fat: 9.8g | Protein: 20.9g | Cholesterol: 93mg

INGREDIENTS

- 1 1/2 pounds ground turkey
- 1 teaspoon salt
- 2 cups dry bread crumbs
- 1 teaspoon pepper
- 1 onion, chopped
- 1 1/2 tablespoons chopped fresh rosemary
- 1 egg, beaten
- 1 cup canned tomato sauce
- 1 cup milk
- 3/4 cup brown sugar
- 1/2 cup balsamic vinegar
- 1 tablespoon Dijon mustard
- 1 clove garlic, minced

DIRECTIONS

1. Preheat oven to 350 degrees F (175 degrees C). Lightly grease a 9x5 inch loaf pan.
2. In a large mixing bowl, mix together the ground turkey, bread crumbs, onion, egg and milk. Season with balsamic vinegar, salt, pepper and rosemary. Press into the prepared pan. Blend together the tomato sauce, brown sugar and mustard; pour evenly over the top of the loaf.
3. Bake for 1 hour in the preheated oven, or until juices run clear when pricked with a knife.

QUINOA WITH CHICKPEAS AND TOMATOES

Servings: 6 | Prep: 20m | Cooks: 20m | Total: 40m

NUTRITION FACTS

Calories: 185 | Carbohydrates: 28.8g | Fat: 5.4g | Protein: 6g | Cholesterol: 0mg

INGREDIENTS

- 1 cup quinoa
- 3 tablespoons lime juice
- 1/8 teaspoon salt
- 4 teaspoons olive oil
- 1 3/4 cups water
- 1/2 teaspoon ground cumin
- 1 cup canned garbanzo beans (chickpeas), drained
- 1 pinch salt and pepper to taste
- 1 tomato, chopped
- 1/2 teaspoon chopped fresh parsley
- 1 clove garlic, minced

DIRECTIONS

1. Place the quinoa in a fine mesh strainer, and rinse under cold, running water until the water no longer foams. Bring the quinoa, salt, and water to a boil in a saucepan. Reduce heat to medium-low, cover, and simmer until the quinoa is tender, 20 to 25 minutes.
2. Once done, stir in the garbanzo beans, tomatoes, garlic, lime juice, and olive oil. Season with cumin, salt, and pepper. Sprinkle with chopped fresh parsley to serve.

LEMON PEPPER GREEN BEANS

Servings: 6 | Prep: 5m | Cooks: 20m | Total: 25m

NUTRITION FACTS

Calories: 81 | Carbohydrates: 6.3g | Fat: 5.9g | Protein: 2.3g | Cholesterol: 10mg

INGREDIENTS

- 1 pound fresh green beans, rinsed and trimmed
- 1/4 cup sliced almonds
- 2 tablespoons butter
- 2 teaspoons lemon pepper

DIRECTIONS

1. Place green beans in a steamer over 1 inch of boiling water. Cover, and cook until tender but still firm, about 10 minutes; drain.
2. Meanwhile, melt butter in a skillet over medium heat. Saute almonds until lightly browned. Season with lemon pepper. Stir in green beans, and toss to coat.

SUGAR SNAP PEAS

Servings: 4 | Prep: 10m | Cooks: 8m | Total: 20m | Additional: 2m

NUTRITION FACTS

Calories: 59 | Carbohydrates: 5.3g | Fat: 3.4g | Protein: 1.4g | Cholesterol: 0mg

INGREDIENTS

- 1/2 pound sugar snap peas
- 1 teaspoon chopped fresh thyme
- 1 tablespoon olive oil
- kosher salt to taste
- 1 tablespoon chopped shallots

DIRECTIONS

1. Preheat oven to 450 degrees F (230 degrees C).
2. Spread sugar snap peas in a single layer on a medium baking sheet, and brush with olive oil. Sprinkle with shallots, thyme, and kosher salt.
3. Bake 6 to 8 minutes in the preheated oven, until tender but firm.

'CHINESE BUFFET' GREEN BEANS

Servings: 6 | Prep: 15m | Cooks: 10m | Total: 25m

NUTRITION FACTS

Calories: 55 | Carbohydrates: 8.1g | Fat: 2.3g | Protein: 1.6g | Cholesterol: 0mg

INGREDIENTS

- 1 tablespoon oil, peanut or sesame
- 1 tablespoon white sugar
- 2 cloves garlic, thinly sliced
- 2 tablespoons oyster sauce

- 1 pound fresh green beans, trimmed
- 2 teaspoons soy sauce

DIRECTIONS

1. Heat peanut oil in a wok or large skillet over medium-high heat. Stir in the garlic, and cook until the edges begin to brown, about 20 seconds. Add the green beans; cook and stir until the green beans begin to soften, about 5 minutes. Stir in the sugar, oyster sauce, and soy sauce. Continue cooking and stirring for several minutes until the beans have attained the desired degree of tenderness.

JAMIE'S SWEET AND EASY CORN ON THE COB

Servings: 6 | Prep: 5m | Cooks: 10m | Total: 15m

NUTRITION FACTS

Calories: 94 | Carbohydrates: 21.5g | Fat: 1.1g | Protein: 2.9g | Cholesterol: 0mg

INGREDIENTS

- 2 tablespoons white sugar
- 6 ears corn on the cob, husks and silk removed
- 1 tablespoon lemon juice

DIRECTIONS

1. Fill a large pot about 3/4 full of water and bring to a boil. Stir in sugar and lemon juice, dissolving the sugar. Gently place ears of corn into boiling water, cover the pot, turn off the heat, and let the corn cook in the hot water until tender, about 10 minutes.

GRILLED STUFFED PORTOBELLO MUSHROOMS

Servings: 4 | Prep: 15m | Cooks: 20m | Total: 35m

NUTRITION FACTS

Calories: 156 | Carbohydrates: 7.3g | Fat: 13.8g | Protein: 3.1g | Cholesterol: 0mg

INGREDIENTS

- 1/2 cup finely chopped red bell pepper
- 1 teaspoon salt
- 1 clove garlic, minced
- 1/2 teaspoon ground black pepper
- 1/4 cup olive oil

- 4 portobello mushroom caps
- 1/4 teaspoon onion powder

DIRECTIONS

1. Preheat grill for medium heat.
2. In a large bowl, mix the red bell pepper, garlic, oil, onion powder, salt, and ground black pepper. Spread mixture over gill side of the mushroom caps.
3. Lightly oil the grill grate. Place mushrooms over indirect heat, cover, and cook for 15 to 20 minutes.

BAKED CHICKEN WITH PEACHES

Servings: 8 | Prep: 15m | Cooks: 30m | Total: 45m

NUTRITION FACTS

Calories: 248 | Carbohydrates: 30.3g | Fat: 2.8g | Protein: 24.6g | Cholesterol: 67mg

INGREDIENTS

- 8 skinless, boneless chicken breast halves
- 1/8 teaspoon ground ginger
- 1 cup brown sugar
- 1/8 teaspoon ground cloves
- 4 fresh peaches - peeled, pitted, and sliced
- 2 tablespoons fresh lemon juice

DIRECTIONS

1. Preheat oven to 350 degrees F (175 degrees C). Lightly grease a 9x13 inch baking dish.
2. Place chicken in the prepared baking dish, and sprinkle with 1/2 cup of brown sugar. Place peach slices over chicken, then sprinkle with remaining 1/2 cup brown sugar, ginger, cloves, and lemon juice.
3. Bake for about 30 minutes in the preheated oven, basting often with juices, until chicken is cooked through and juices run clear.

SLOW COOKER CHICKEN WITH MUSHROOM WINE SAUCE

Servings: 4 | Prep: 10m | Cooks: 6h | Total: 6h10m

NUTRITION FACTS

Calories: 208 | Carbohydrates: 7.6g | Fat: 7.1g | Protein: 24.9g | Cholesterol: 61mg

INGREDIENTS

- 1 (10.75 ounce) can condensed cream of mushroom soup
- 1 tablespoon milk
- 1 teaspoon dried minced onion
- 1 (4 ounce) can mushroom pieces, drained
- 1 teaspoon dried parsley
- salt and pepper to taste
- 1/4 cup white wine
- 4 boneless, skinless chicken breast halves
- 1/4 teaspoon garlic powder

DIRECTIONS

1. In a slow cooker, mix together the soup, onion, parsley, wine, garlic powder, milk, and mushroom pieces. Season with salt and pepper. Place chicken in the slow cooker, covering with the soup mixture.
2. Cook on Low setting for 5 to 6 hours, or on High setting for 3 to 4 hours.

CHINESE PORK CHOPS

Servings: 6 | Prep: 15m | Cooks: 15m | Total: 8h30m | Additional: 8h

NUTRITION FACTS

Calories: 182 | Carbohydrates: 11.2g | Fat: 6.3g | Protein: 19.6g | Cholesterol: 48mg

INGREDIENTS

- 1/2 cup soy sauce
- 1/2 teaspoon ground ginger
- 1/4 cup brown sugar
- 1/8 teaspoon garlic powder
- 2 tablespoons lemon juice
- 6 boneless pork chops
- 1 tablespoon vegetable oil

DIRECTIONS

1. In a bowl, mix the soy sauce, brown sugar, lemon juice, vegetable oil, ginger, and garlic powder. Set aside some of the mixture in a separate bowl for marinating during cooking. Pierce the pork chops on both sides with a fork, place in a large resealable plastic bag, and cover with the remaining marinade mixture. Refrigerate 6 to 8 hours.

2. Preheat the grill for high heat.

3. Lightly oil the grill grate. Discard marinade, and grill pork chops 6 to 8 minutes per side, or to desired doneness, marinating often with the reserved portion of the marinade.

FABULOUS FRIED CABBAGE

Servings: 6 | Prep: 5m | Cooks: 45m | Total: 50m

NUTRITION FACTS

Calories: 66 | Carbohydrates: 11.8g | Fat: 1.7g | Protein: 2.9g | Cholesterol: 5mg

INGREDIENTS

- 2 teaspoons butter
- 1 head cabbage, cored and coarsely chopped
- 1 (15 ounce) can chicken broth
- 1 pinch salt and pepper to taste

DIRECTIONS

1. Bring the butter and chicken broth to a boil in a large skillet. Reduce heat to low and add the cabbage. Cover and cook over low heat to steam the cabbage for about 45 minutes, stirring frequently, or until cabbage is tender and sweet. Season with salt and pepper and serve..

SLOW COOKER CHICKEN CREOLE

Servings: 4 | Prep: 10m | Cooks: 12h | Total: 12h10m

NUTRITION FACTS

Calories: 189 | Carbohydrates: 13.8g | Fat: 1.9g | Protein: 29.6g | Cholesterol: 68mg

INGREDIENTS

- 4 skinless, boneless chicken breast halves
- 1 green bell pepper, diced
- salt and pepper to taste
- 3 cloves garlic, minced
- Creole-style seasoning to taste
- 1 onion, diced
- 1 (14.5 ounce) can stewed tomatoes, with liquid
- 1 (4 ounce) can mushrooms, drained
- 1 stalk celery, diced

* 1 fresh jalapeno pepper, seeded and chopped

DIRECTIONS

1. Place chicken breasts in slow cooker. Season with salt, pepper, and Creole-style seasoning to taste. Stir in tomatoes with liquid, celery, bell pepper, garlic, onion, mushrooms, and jalapeno pepper.
2. Cook on Low for 10 to 12 hours, or on High for 5 to 6 hours.

MOROCCAN CHICKEN

Servings: 4 | Prep: 10m | Cooks: 30m | Total: 45m | Additional: 5m

NUTRITION FACTS

Calories: 286 | Carbohydrates: 27.9g | Fat: 3.7g | Protein: 36g | Cholesterol: 67mg

INGREDIENTS

* 1 pound skinless, boneless chicken breast meat - cubed
* 1/2 teaspoon dried oregano
* 2 teaspoons salt
* 1/4 teaspoon ground cayenne pepper
* 1 onion, chopped
* 1/4 teaspoon ground turmeric
* 2 cloves garlic, chopped
* 1 1/2 cups chicken broth
* 2 carrots, sliced
* 1 cup crushed tomatoes
* 2 stalks celery, sliced
* 1 cup canned chickpeas, drained
* 1 tablespoon minced fresh ginger root
* 1 zucchini, sliced
* 1/2 teaspoon paprika
* 1 tablespoon lemon juice
* 3/4 teaspoon ground cumin

DIRECTIONS

1. Season chicken with salt and brown in a large saucepan over medium heat until almost cooked through. Remove chicken from pan and set aside.
2. Saute onion, garlic, carrots and celery in same pan. When tender, stir in ginger, paprika, cumin, oregano, cayenne pepper and turmeric; stir fry for about 1 minute, then mix in broth and tomatoes. Return chicken to pan, reduce heat to low and simmer for about 10 minutes.

3. Add chickpeas and zucchini to pan and bring to simmering once again; cover pan and cook for about 15 minutes, or until zucchini is cooked through and tender. Stir in lemon juice and serve.

SPICY BASIL CHICKEN

Servings: 4 | Prep: 15m | Cooks: 15m | Total: 30m

NUTRITION FACTS

Calories: 244 | Carbohydrates: 11.9g | Fat: 9.4g | Protein: 28.2g | Cholesterol: 69mg

INGREDIENTS

- 2 tablespoons chili oil
- 1 teaspoon black pepper
- 2 cloves garlic
- 5 tablespoons oyster sauce
- 3 hot chile peppers
- 1 cup fresh mushrooms
- 1 pound skinless, boneless chicken breast halves - cut into bite-size pieces
- 1 cup chopped onions
- 1 1/2 teaspoons white sugar
- 1 bunch fresh basil leaves
- 1 teaspoon garlic salt

DIRECTIONS

1. Heat the oil in a skillet over medium-high heat, and cook the garlic and chile peppers until golden brown. Mix in chicken and sugar, and season with garlic salt and pepper. Cook until chicken is no longer pink, but not done.
2. Stir oyster sauce into the skillet. Mix in mushrooms and onions, and continue cooking until onions are tender and chicken juices run clear. Remove from heat, and mix in basil. Let sit 2 minutes before serving.

FRIED ONION RINGS

Servings: 12 | Prep: 15m | Cooks: 20m | Total: 45m | Additional: 10m

NUTRITION FACTS

Calories: 126 | Carbohydrates: 11.9g | Fat: 7.5g | Protein: 1.6g | Cholesterol: 0mg

INGREDIENTS

- 1 quart vegetable oil for frying
- 1 pinch salt
- 1 cup all-purpose flour
- 1 pinch ground black pepper
- 1 cup beer
- 4 onions, peeled and sliced into rings

DIRECTIONS

1. In a large, deep skillet, heat oil to 365 degrees F (180 degrees C).
2. In a medium bowl, combine flour, beer, salt, and pepper. Mix until smooth. Dredge onion slices in the batter, until evenly coated. Deep fry in the hot oil until golden brown. Drain on paper towels.

CRISPY CUCUMBERS AND TOMATOES IN DILL DRESSING

Servings: 6 | Prep: 15m | Cooks: 15m | Total: 30m

NUTRITION FACTS

Calories: 71 | Carbohydrates: 6.7g | Fat: 4.7g | Protein: 1g | Cholesterol: 0mg

INGREDIENTS

- 1/4 cup cider vinegar
- 2 tablespoons vegetable oil
- 1 teaspoon white sugar
- 2 cucumbers, sliced
- 1/2 teaspoon salt
- 1 cup sliced red onion
- 1/2 teaspoon chopped fresh dill weed
- 2 ripe tomatoes, cut into wedges
- 1/4 teaspoon ground black pepper

DIRECTIONS

1. In a large bowl, mix the vinegar, sugar, salt, dill, pepper, and oil. Add cucumbers, onion, and tomatoes. Toss, and let stand at least 15 minutes before serving.

CHICKEN BROCCOLI CA - UNIENG'S STYLE

Servings: 6 | Prep: 10m | Cooks: 25m | Total: 35m

Calories: 170 | Carbohydrates: 9.8g | Fat: 7.9g | Protein: 16.2g | Cholesterol: 33mg

INGREDIENTS

- 12 ounces boneless, skinless chicken breast halves, cut into bite-sized pieces
- 1/2 cup water
- 1 tablespoon oyster sauce
- 1 teaspoon ground black pepper
- 2 tablespoons dark soy sauce
- 1 teaspoon white sugar
- 3 tablespoons vegetable oil
- 1/2 medium head bok choy, chopped
- 2 cloves garlic, chopped
- 1 small head broccoli, chopped
- 1 large onion, cut into rings
- 1 tablespoon cornstarch, mixed with equal parts water

DIRECTIONS

1. In a large bowl, combine chicken, oyster sauce and soy sauce. Set aside for 15 minutes.
2. Heat oil in a wok or large heavy skillet over medium heat. Saute garlic and onion until soft and translucent. Increase heat to high. Add chicken and marinade, then stir-fry until light golden brown, about 10 minutes. Stir in water, pepper and sugar. Add bok choy and broccoli, and cook stirring until soft, about 10 minutes. Pour in the cornstarch mixture, and cook until sauce is thickened, about 5 minutes.

PATTI'S MUSSELS A LA MARINIERE
Servings: 6 | Prep: 10m | Cooks: 15m | Total: 25m

NUTRITION FACTS

Calories: 161 | Carbohydrates: 5.7g | Fat: 8.7g | Protein: 7.7g | Cholesterol: 18mg

INGREDIENTS

- 50 fresh mussels, scrubbed and debearded
- 3 green onions, chopped
- 2 tablespoons extra virgin olive oil
- 1 bunch fresh parsley, chopped
- 5 cloves garlic, minced
- 3 roma (plum) tomatoes, chopped

- 1 cup white wine
- salt and pepper to taste
- 2 tablespoons margarine or butter

DIRECTIONS

1. Place mussels in a large bowl with cold water to cover. Let them soak for about 20 minutes to remove any dirt or sand.
2. Heat olive oil in a large stockpot over medium-low heat. Add garlic, and saute for one minute, but do not brown. Add the chopped green onion and tomatoes, and cook until almost tender. Pour in the white wine, and stir in the parsley and butter. Bring to a boil, and allow to boil until the liquid has reduced by half, about 15 minutes. Season with salt and pepper to taste.
3. Add the mussels to the pot, cover and allow to cook until the shells are opened, about 10 minutes. Transfer the mussels and sauce to a large serving bowl, discarding any unopened shells. Bon appetit!

SPICY TUNA FISH CAKES

Servings: 4 | Prep: 20m | Cooks: 30m | Total: 50m

NUTRITION FACTS

Calories: 237 | Carbohydrates: 20.7g | Fat: 5.6g | Protein: 25.2g | Cholesterol: 72mg

INGREDIENTS

- 1 large potato, peeled and cubed
- 1 1/2 teaspoons garlic powder
- 4 (3 ounce) cans tuna, drained
- 1 teaspoon Italian seasoning
- 1 egg
- 1/4 teaspoon cayenne pepper
- 1/4 cup chopped onion
- salt and ground black pepper to taste
- 1 tablespoon Dijon mustard
- 1 tablespoon olive oil
- 1 tablespoon dry breadcrumbs, or as needed

DIRECTIONS

1. Place the potato into a small pot and cover with salted water. Bring to a boil over high heat, then reduce heat to medium-low, cover, and simmer until tender, about 20 minutes. Drain and allow to steam dry for a minute or two, then mash the potato with a potato masher or fork in a large bowl.
2. Mix the tuna, egg, onion, Dijon mustard, bread crumbs, garlic powder, Italian seasoning, cayenne pepper, salt, and pepper into the mashed potato until well-blended. Divide the tuna mixture into 8 equal portions and shape into patties.

3. Heat the olive oil in a skillet over medium heat. Pan fry the tuna patties until browned and crisp, about 3 minutes on each side.

TEXAS CAVIAR

Servings: 16 | Prep: 15m | Cooks: 1h | Total: 1h15m | Additional: 1h

NUTRITION FACTS

Calories: 107 | Carbohydrates: 11.8g | Fat: 5.4g | Protein: 3.5g | Cholesterol: 0mg

INGREDIENTS

- 1/2 onion, chopped
- 1 (8 ounce) bottle zesty Italian dressing
- 1 green bell pepper, chopped
- 1 (15 ounce) can black beans, drained
- 1 bunch green onions, chopped
- 1 (15 ounce) can black-eyed peas, drained
- 2 jalapeno peppers, chopped
- 1/2 teaspoon ground coriander
- 1 tablespoon minced garlic
- 1 bunch chopped fresh cilantro
- 1 pint cherry tomatoes, quartered

DIRECTIONS

1. In a large bowl, mix together onion, green bell pepper, green onions, jalapeno peppers, garlic, cherry tomatoes, zesty Italian dressing, black beans, black-eyed peas and coriander. Cover and chill in the refrigerator approximately 2 hours. Toss with desired amount of fresh cilantro to serve.

FRESH STRAWBERRY PIE

Servings: 16 | Prep: 15m | Cooks: 15m | Total: 2h30m | Additional: 2h

NUTRITION FACTS

Calories: 167 | Carbohydrates: 31.6g | Fat: 4.4g | Protein: 1.7g | Cholesterol: 0mg

INGREDIENTS

- 2 (8 inch) pie shells, baked
- 2 tablespoons cornstarch
- 2 1/2 quarts fresh strawberries
- 1 cup boiling water

- 1 cup white sugar
- 1 (3 ounce) package strawberry flavored Jell-O

DIRECTIONS

1. In a saucepan, mix together the sugar and corn starch; make sure to blend corn starch in completely. Add boiling water, and cook over medium heat until mixture thickens. Remove from heat. Add gelatin mix, and stir until smooth. Let mixture cool to room temperature.
2. Place strawberries in baked pie shells; position berries with points facing up. Pour cooled gel mixture over strawberries.
3. Refrigerate until set. Serve with whipped cream, if desired.

ALFREDO LIGHT

Servings: 8 | Prep: 20m | Cooks: 20m | Total: 40m

NUTRITION FACTS

Calories: 292 | Carbohydrates: 50.5g | Fat: 4.1g | Protein: 13.9g | Cholesterol: 6mg

INGREDIENTS

- 1 onion, chopped
- 1/2 teaspoon salt
- 1 clove garlic, minced
- 1/4 teaspoon ground black pepper
- 2 teaspoons vegetable oil
- 1/2 cup grated Parmesan cheese
- 2 cups skim milk
- 16 ounces dry fettuccine pasta
- 1 cup chicken broth
- 1 (16 ounce) package frozen broccoli florets
- 3 tablespoons all-purpose flour

DIRECTIONS

1. In a medium saucepan, heat oil over medium heat. Add onion and garlic, and saute until golden brown.
2. In a small saucepan, stir together milk, chicken broth, flour, salt and pepper over low heat until smooth and thick. Stir into onion mixture. Continue to cook over medium low heat, stirring frequently, until the sauce is thick. Stir in Parmesan cheese.
3. Meanwhile, cook pasta in boiling water. Add broccoli to the pasta for the last several minutes of cooking. Continue cooking until the pasta is al dente.
4. Drain the pasta and vegetables, and transfer to a large bowl. Toss with sauce. Serve.

SPICY BLACK BEAN CAKES

Servings: 8 | Prep: 20m | Cooks: 15m | Total: 35m

NUTRITION FACTS

Calories: 219 | Carbohydrates: 31.3g | Fat: 6.7g | Protein: 9.4g | Cholesterol: 29mg

INGREDIENTS

- 1/2 cup reduced fat sour cream
- 2 fresh jalapeno peppers, finely diced
- 2 teaspoons fresh lime juice
- 1 tablespoon ground cumin
- 1 small fresh jalapeno pepper, minced
- 2 (14.5 ounce) cans black beans, drained and rinsed
- salt to taste
- salt and black pepper to taste
- 2 tablespoons olive oil, divided
- 2 cups grated raw sweet potato
- 4 green onions, thinly sliced
- 1 egg, lightly beaten
- 6 cloves garlic, pressed
- 1/2 cup plain dried bread crumbs

DIRECTIONS

1. To prepare lime sour cream, mix the sour cream, lime juice, 1 small minced jalapeno, and salt together in a small bowl. Cover, and refrigerate.
2. Heat 1 tablespoon olive oil in a small skillet over medium heat. Cook green onions until softened, about 1 minute. Stir in garlic, 2 diced jalapenos, and cumin; cook until fragrant, about 30 seconds.
3. Transfer contents of skillet to a large bowl. Stir in black beans, and mash with a fork. Season with salt and pepper to taste. Mix in sweet potatoes, egg, and bread crumbs. Divide into 8 balls, and flatten into patties.
4. In the oven, set cooking rack about 4 inches from heat source. Set oven to broil. Lightly grease baking sheet with 1 tablespoon oil.
5. Place bean patties on baking sheet, and broil 8 to 10 minutes. Turn cakes over, and broil until crispy, about 3 minutes more. Serve with lime sour cream.

EASIEST EGGPLANT

Servings: 6 | Prep: 10m | Cooks: 45m | Total: 55m

NUTRITION FACTS

Calories: 126 | Carbohydrates: 12.3g | Fat: 8g | Protein: 2.4g | Cholesterol: 4mg

INGREDIENTS

- 1 medium eggplant, peeled and sliced into 1/2 inch rounds
- 1/2 cup seasoned bread crumbs
- 4 tablespoons mayonnaise, or as needed

DIRECTIONS

1. Preheat the oven to 350 degrees F. Line a baking sheet with aluminum foil.
2. Place the bread crumbs in a shallow dish. Coat each slice of eggplant on both sides with mayonnaise. Press into the bread crumbs to coat. Place coated eggplant slices on the prepared baking sheet.
3. Bake for 20 minutes in the preheated oven, until golden brown. Flip slices over, and cook for an additional 20 to 25 minutes to brown the other side.

AUNT JEWEL'S CHICKEN DRESSING CASSEROLE

Servings: 12 | Prep: 15m | Cooks: 45m | Total: 1h

NUTRITION FACTS

Calories: 236 | Carbohydrates: 15.8g | Fat: 5.2g | Protein: 29.5g | Cholesterol: 73mg

INGREDIENTS

- 3 pounds skinless, boneless chicken breast meat
- 1 (10.75 ounce) can milk
- 1 (10.75 ounce) can condensed cream of chicken soup
- 1 1/2 cups chicken broth
- 1 (10.75 ounce) can condensed cream of celery soup
- 1 (6 ounce) package seasoned cornbread stuffing mix

DIRECTIONS

1. Place chicken in a large saucepan full of lightly salted water. Bring to a boil; boil for about 30 minutes, or until chicken is cooked through (juices run clear). Remove chicken from pan, reserving broth. Cut chicken into bite size pieces and place in bottom of a 9x13 inch baking dish.
2. Preheat oven to 350 degrees F (175 degrees C).
3. In a medium bowl mix together cream of chicken soup and cream of celery soup. Fill one empty soup can with milk, and mix milk with soups. Pour mixture over chicken. In a small bowl combine stuffing and broth; mix together and spoon mixture over casserole.
4. Bake in the preheated oven for 45 minutes.

CUCUMBER SUNOMONO

Servings: 5 | Prep: 15m | Cooks: 1h | Total: 1h15m

NUTRITION FACTS

Calories: 27 | Carbohydrates: 6.2 g | Fat: 0.2g | Protein: 0.6g | Cholesterol: 0mg

INGREDIENTS

- 2 large cucumbers, peeled
- 1 teaspoon salt
- 1/3 cup rice vinegar
- 1 1/2 teaspoons minced fresh ginger root
- 4 teaspoons white sugar

DIRECTIONS

1. Cut cucumbers in half lengthwise and scoop out any large seeds. Slice crosswise into very thin slices.
2. In a small bowl combine vinegar, sugar, salt and ginger. Mix well. Place cucumbers inside of the bowl, stir so that cucumbers are coated with the mixture. Refrigerate the bowl of cucumbers for at least 1 hour before serving.

STEWED CABBAGE

Servings: 4 | Prep: 15m | Cooks: 40m | Total: 55m

NUTRITION FACTS

Calories: 200 | Carbohydrates: 23.1g | Fat: 11.9g | Protein: 4.4g | Cholesterol: 31mg

INGREDIENTS

- 1/4 cup butter
- 1 medium head cabbage, cut into squares
- 2 onions, chopped
- 1 (14.5 ounce) can stewed tomatoes, with liquid
- 1 stalk celery, chopped
- salt and pepper to taste
- 2 cloves garlic, chopped

DIRECTIONS

1. Melt butter in a large saucepan over medium heat. Add onion, celery, and garlic and saute for 3 to 5 minutes, or until translucent. Stir in cabbage, reduce heat to low, and simmer for 15 minutes.

2. Pour in tomatoes and season with salt and pepper to taste. Cover pan and cook over medium heat for 30 to 40 minutes, or until cabbage is tender.

OVEN FRIES

Servings: 6 | Prep: 15m | Cooks: 30m | Total: 45m

NUTRITION FACTS

Calories: 156 | Carbohydrates: 34.1g | Fat: 1g | Protein: 3.8g | Cholesterol: 0mg

INGREDIENTS

- 2 1/2 pounds baking potatoes
- 1 teaspoon salt
- 1 teaspoon vegetable oil
- 1 pinch ground cayenne pepper
- 1 tablespoon white sugar

DIRECTIONS

1. Preheat oven to 450 degrees F (230 degrees C). Line a baking sheet with foil, and coat well with vegetable cooking spray. Scrub potatoes well and cut into 1/2 inch thick fries.
2. In a large mixing bowl, toss potatoes with oil, sugar, salt and red pepper. Spread on baking sheet in one layer.
3. Bake for 30 minutes in the preheated oven, until potatoes are tender and browned. Serve immediately.

SAUTEED PORTOBELLOS AND SPINACH

Servings: 4 | Prep: 10m | Cooks: 10m | Total: 20m

NUTRITION FACTS

Calories: 146 | Carbohydrates: 6.6g | Fat: 11g | Protein: 6.6g | Cholesterol: 28mg

INGREDIENTS

- 3 tablespoons butter
- 1/4 teaspoon black pepper
- 2 large portobello mushrooms, sliced
- 1 clove garlic, chopped
- 1 (10 ounce) package frozen chopped spinach, thawed and drained
- 2 tablespoons dry red wine

- 1/4 teaspoon dried basil
- 1/4 cup grated Parmesan cheese
- 1/4 teaspoon salt

DIRECTIONS

1. Melt butter in a large skillet or saute pan over medium heat. Saute mushrooms, spinach, basil, salt, pepper and garlic until mushrooms are tender and spinach is heated through.
2. Pour in wine and reduce heat to low; simmer 1 minute. Stir in Parmesan cheese and serve.

HOT AND SOUR CHINESE EGGPLANT

Servings: 4 | Prep: 30m | Cooks: 5m | Total: 35m

NUTRITION FACTS

Calories: 153 | Carbohydrates: 21.1g | Fat: 7.8g | Protein: 3.4g | Cholesterol: 0mg

INGREDIENTS

- 2 long Chinese eggplants, cubed
- 1 teaspoon cornstarch
- 1 1/2 tablespoons soy sauce
- 1/2 teaspoon chili oil, or to taste
- 1 tablespoon red wine vinegar
- 2 teaspoons salt
- 1 tablespoon white sugar
- 2 tablespoons vegetable oil
- 1 green chile pepper, chopped

DIRECTIONS

1. Place the eggplant cubes into a large bowl, and sprinkle with salt. Fill with enough water to cover, and let stand for 30 minutes. Rinse well, and drain on paper towels.
2. In a small bowl, stir together the soy sauce, red wine vinegar, sugar, chile pepper, cornstarch and chili oil. Set the sauce aside.
3. Heat the vegetable oil in a large skillet or wok over medium-high heat. Fry the eggplant until it is tender and begins to brown, 5 to 10 minutes. Pour in the sauce, and cook and stir until the sauce is thick and the eggplant is evenly coated. Serve immediately.